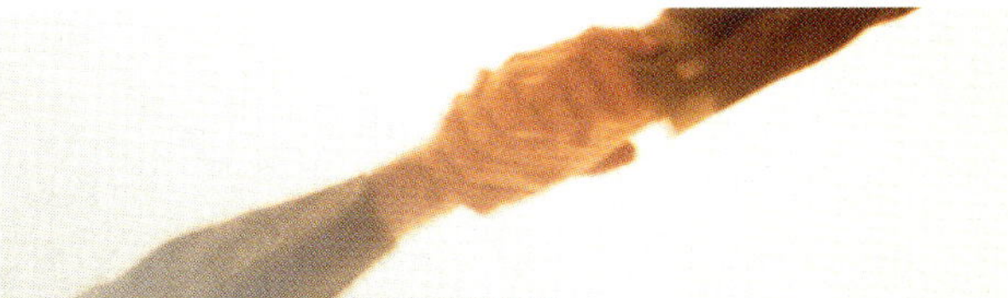

TO THE DIRECTOR

This student folder contains nine study leaflets and the enrichment magazine. Remove the middle staple and distribute the leaflets as indicated in the leaders guide. This magazine should be distributed at the first session for use throughout the course.

3558 S. Jefferson Ave, St. Louis, MO 63118-3968
1-800-325-3040 • www.cph.org

Written by Robert C. Baker

Edited by Edward Engelbrecht

This publication may be available in braille, in large print, or on cassette tape for the visually impaired. Please allow 8 to 12 weeks for delivery. Write to the Library for the Blind, 7550 Watson Rd., St. Louis, MO 63119-4409; call toll-free 1-888-215-2455; or visit the Web site: www.blindmission.org.

Cover illustration by Steven Noble
Graphic design by Lesley Rusick and Karen Pauls

Manufactured in the U.S.A.

ENRICHMENT MAGAZINE

IN THIS ISSUE

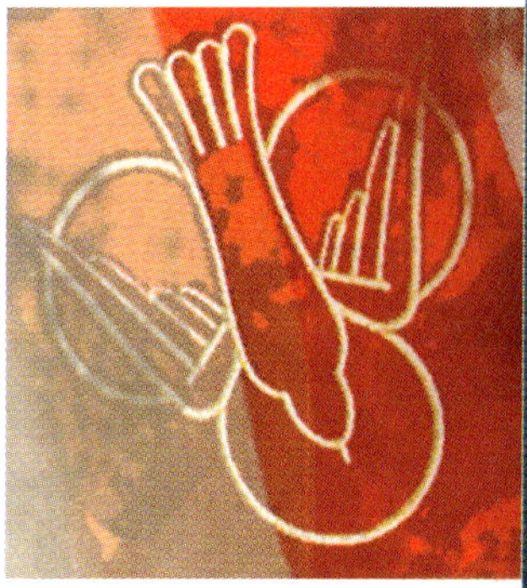

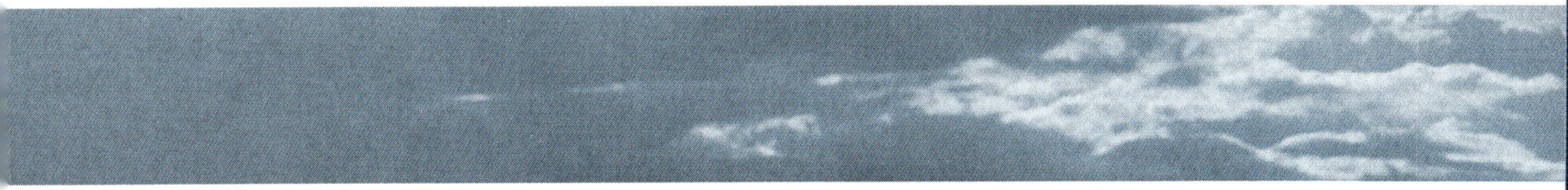

Paul's Example

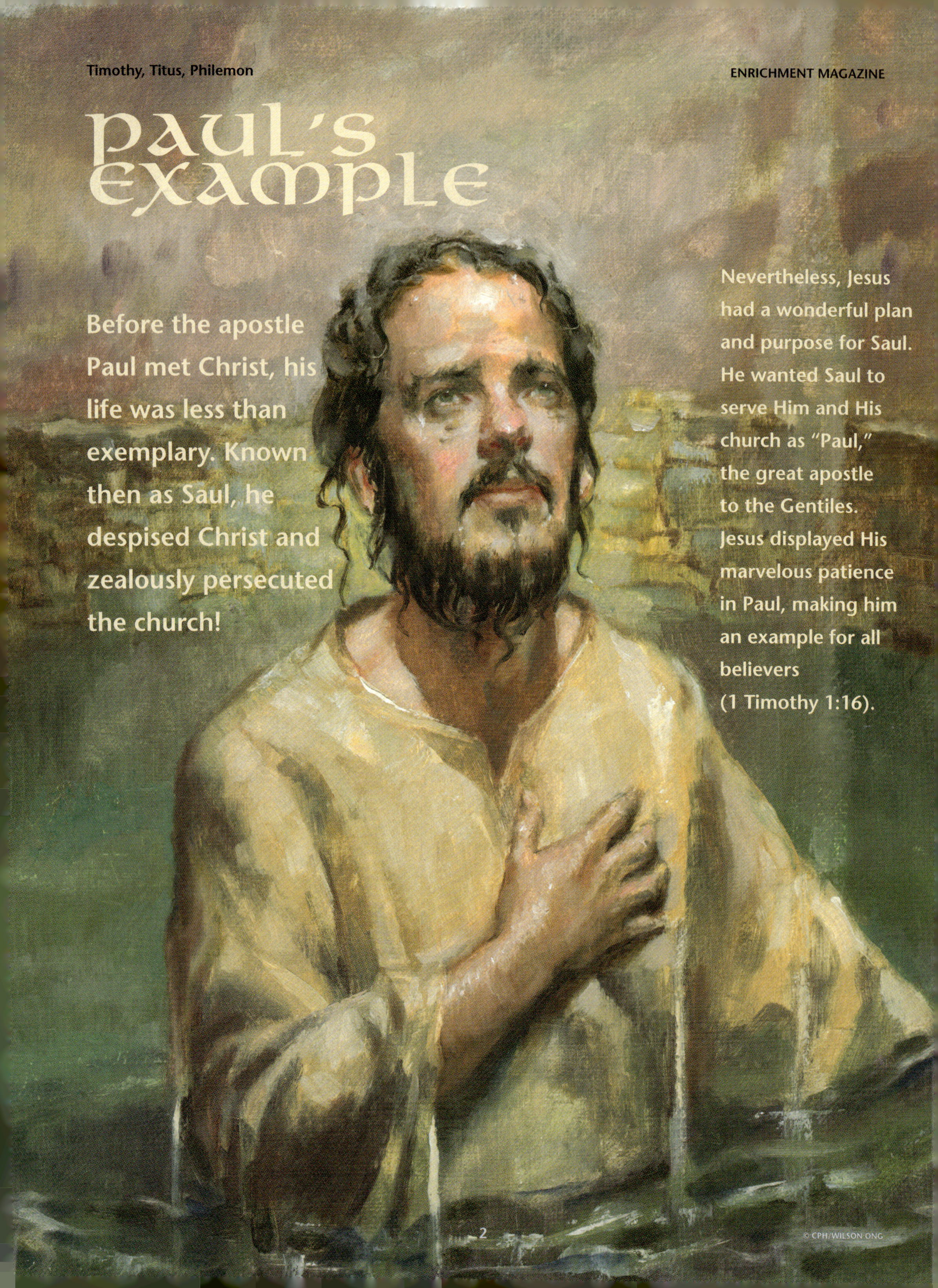

Before the apostle Paul met Christ, his life was less than exemplary. Known then as Saul, he despised Christ and zealously persecuted the church!

Nevertheless, Jesus had a wonderful plan and purpose for Saul. He wanted Saul to serve Him and His church as "Paul," the great apostle to the Gentiles. Jesus displayed His marvelous patience in Paul, making him an example for all believers (1 Timothy 1:16).

The "Foremost" Sinner

Before that day on the Damascus Road (Acts 9:1–9), Saul considered himself a righteous, God-fearing person. He was "circumcised on the eighth day, of the people of Israel, of the tribe of Benjamin, a Hebrew of Hebrews; as to the law, a Pharisee" (Philippians 3:5). Saul believed his relationship with God was established through his family heritage and his own strict observance of the Law. He boasted about both his religious upbringing and his "good deeds," serving as an example for others to follow. In his religious fervor Saul had even persuaded himself that God called him to persecute Christians, those who "blasphemed" God by claiming Jesus was God's Son.

> I myself was convinced that I ought to do many things in opposing the name of Jesus of Nazareth. And I did so in Jerusalem. I not only locked up many of the saints in prison after receiving authority from the chief priests, but when they were put to death I cast my vote against them. And I punished them often in all the synagogues and tried to make them blaspheme, and in raging fury against them I persecuted them even to foreign cities. (Acts 26:9–11)

Unknowing and unbelieving, Saul participated in the imprisonment and murder of Christian believers. In God's eyes, Saul was "foremost" among sinners. Later, by the power of God's Spirit working through the Word, Saul would come to realize that about himself. But Saul was not one of the worst of sinners due to lack of works. Saul abounded in "good works," at least in his own eyes and the eyes of his peers. Rather, Saul was among the "foremost" sinners due to his lack of faith, his rejection of God's only begotten Son. Jesus confronted Saul and changed his life, and more, forever.

Jesus Included Paul among the Saints

Jesus' appearance on the Damascus Road transformed Saul's life. As the apostle recalled later, a bright light from heaven appeared and flashed all around him. He was stricken to the ground. Although his traveling companions could see the light, they could not hear the Voice speaking to Saul. The Voice called out Saul's name and asked why he was attacking His body, the church. Saul needed to know who was speaking, so he asked the Voice to declare itself. The Voice said, "I am Jesus of Nazareth, whom you are persecuting" (Acts 22:8).

The flashing light blinded Saul. Yet, Jesus instructed him to continue his journey to Damascus and to seek out Ananias, one of the Lord's disciples. Before Saul arrived, Jesus prepared Ananias for Saul's visit by saying, "Go, for he [Saul] is a chosen instrument of Mine to carry My name before the Gentiles and kings and the children of Israel" (Acts 9:15). After Saul arrived, Jesus worked through Ananias to restore Saul's physical sight. He also restored Saul's spiritual sight through a miraculous washing. Later, when confessing his faith before a Jerusalem crowd, he remembered Ananias saying these words:

> The God of our fathers appointed you to know His will, to see the Righteous One and to hear a voice from His mouth; for you will be a witness for Him to everyone of what you have seen and heard. And now why do you wait? Rise and be baptized and wash away your sins, calling on His name. (Acts 22:14–16)

Ananias baptized Saul. Receiving God's triune name, Saul took on a new name too: Paul. After persecuting God's people, Saul believed in the name of Jesus. He would bless God's people by proclaiming the name of Jesus. With his sight restored, Paul could surely sing the phrase, " 'Twas blind, but now I see!" Out of His love and grace, Jesus gave both physical and spiritual sight to Paul. Indeed, the Lord had transformed the "foremost" among sinners into one of His chosen saints!

Jesus Displayed His Patience in Paul

Why did God select someone like Saul? Why did God go to such lengths to transform him into "a servant of Christ Jesus, called to be an apostle, set apart for the gospel of God" (Romans 1:1)? Paul tells us the reason:

> The saying is trustworthy and deserving of full acceptance, that Christ Jesus came into the world to save sinners, of whom I am the foremost. But I received mercy for this reason, that in me, as the foremost, Jesus Christ might display His perfect patience as an example to those who were to believe in Him for eternal life. (1 Timothy 1:15–16)

God is patient, "not wishing that any should perish, but that all should reach repentance" (2 Peter 3:9). God patiently waits for sinners to repent of their sins, giving them the gift of faith in His Son, Jesus of Nazareth. God selected Paul to serve as an example of His patience at work in our hearts.

Paul's immediate experience with Christ and his dramatic conversion are not typical for every believer. But for everyone baptized into the triune name, Christ comes just as powerfully and just as dramatically to restore our spiritual eyesight. Everyone baptized in the triune name encounters a loving and forgiving God who earnestly desires "all people to be saved and to come to the knowledge of the truth" (1 Timothy 2:4). By water and the Word, Jesus has called each of us by His name to follow Him.

Jesus Makes You His Example

Like Saul, you, too, act in ignorance and unbelief when you fall into sin. Sometimes, even when you do not suspect it, your words and deeds hurt others and bring discredit to our Lord. More frequently, you disobey God by breaking His Ten Commandments. We all allow our sinful pride to take control, even persuading ourselves that we are accomplishing "the Lord's work." Feeling justified because we're doing something in God's name, we may cause real harm to Christ's body through our sinful words and deeds. We become a bad example to others! After his dramatic conversion, Paul still wrestled with his sinful flesh: "So I find it to be a law that when I want to do right, evil lies close at hand. . . . Wretched man that I am! Who will deliver me from this body of death?" (Romans 7:21, 24).

But like Paul, the forgiven saint, you can exclaim, "Thanks be to God through Jesus Christ our Lord!" (7:25). The same Lord that met and transformed Saul into Paul continues meeting and transforming you through His Word spoken or read, your Baptism, the words of Absolution, and through His own Holy Meal. Richly forgiving your sins in Christ, God's Spirit is now conforming you "to the image of His Son, in order that He might be the firstborn among many brothers" (Romans 8:29). God gave you Paul as an example of His amazing patience and of His marvelous and forgiving grace. In Christ, God showers you with His grace so that others can see Him at work in you. In this way, you are an example of God's patience, just like Paul.

The Central Message

"Christ Jesus came into the world to save sinners" (1 Timothy 1:15).

Often God's Word describes terrible consequences for disobeying God's Law. It also prescribes proper behavior. And yet, this is only part of what Scripture tells us. Its pages are also filled with Good News, which provide peace, comfort, hope, and joy. Its message is one of God's love and forgiveness through His Son. Jesus Himself said, "I came not to call the righteous, but sinners" (Matthew 9:13), and "the Son of Man came to seek and to save the lost" (Luke 19:10).

Paul's Letters to Timothy, Titus, and Philemon are like the whole Bible in that they contain both Law and Gospel. In his Letters Paul warns and he commands. He gives apostolic instructions regarding worship, church teaching, the conduct of church leaders and laypersons, and relationships within the family and at work. He also makes practical requests. These things are important. But throughout his writings to church leaders, Paul always comes back to the Bible's central message: God saves you in Jesus Christ.

God Our Savior

At first glance the Pastoral Epistles (1, 2 Timothy and Titus), as well as Paul's Letter to Philemon, might appear simply as rules and regulations Paul expects his recipients to follow. But look more closely. Paul begins his First Letter to Timothy with words that will show up again and again in his Letters: "Paul, an apostle of Christ Jesus by command of God our Savior and of Christ Jesus our hope" (1 Timothy 1:1, emphasis added). Paul will use the phrase "God our Savior," or one similar to it, twice more in this Letter (2:3; 4:10). He will also write it three times in his Letter to Titus (1:3; 2:10; 3:4).

Further, Paul refers not only to God the Father but also God the Son, as Savior:

> [This grace] which He gave us in Christ Jesus before the ages began, and which now has been manifested through the appearing of our Savior Christ Jesus, who abolished death and brought life and immortality to light through the gospel. (2 Timothy 1:9–10)

"Christ Jesus our Savior" will appear three times in Paul's Letter to Titus (1:4; 2:13; 3:6).

Challenges, Challenges

Paul reminds his original readers (and all of us today!) of the central message recorded in God's Word: God's wonderful saving activity through His Son, Jesus Christ. Why would that be so important for his original readers and for us?

To start, it is helpful to remember that Timothy was Paul's younger disciple. Timothy's father was a Greek pagan. Timothy's Jewish Christian mother and grandmother taught him the Old Testament Scriptures (2 Timothy 1:5; 3:14–15). Paul led Timothy to Christ (1 Timothy 1:2), and Timothy served with Paul in his missionary efforts in Macedonia, Achaia, Ephesus, and elsewhere (see Acts 17:14–15; 18:5; 19:22; 20:1–6). Titus, too, was converted by Paul (Titus 1:4) and faithfully served him as a coworker in bringing the Gospel to the Gentiles (see Galatians 2:1–3; Titus 1:5; 2:15; 3:12–13). He was also sent to Dalmatia (modern-day Albania) as Paul's delegate (2 Timothy 4:10). And while the Bible does not detail how Philemon came to faith, it is evident that he was a man of some means, for a congregation met in his home (Philemon 1:2).

Timothy, Titus, and Philemon each had challenges as they joined Paul in service to the church. Paul encouraged Timothy to remain faithful to his calling in spite of age discrimination (1 Timothy 4:12–13). He urged Titus to set a good example for other believers (Titus 2:7–8), many of whom were either older (2:2, 3) or younger (2:4, 6). Paul exhorted Philemon, his "partner" in the Gospel (v. 17), to change his attitude toward his runaway slave and welcome him back (vv. 17, 21). And yet, these three church leaders also needed to hear that the message of Good News always applied to them in spite of hardship (Romans 8:33–39), instruction (2 Timothy 3:16–17), and correction (Job 5:17–18).

More Good News

The Good News was also for them! They, too, could take comfort in knowing that God saves us in Christ. The story of Jesus pervades Paul's Letters to Timothy, Titus, and Philemon:

> For there is one God, and there is one mediator between God and men, the man Christ Jesus, who gave Himself as a ransom for all. (1 Timothy 2:5–6)

> [This grace] which He gave us in Christ Jesus before the ages began, and which now has been manifested through the appearing of our Savior Christ Jesus, who abolished death and brought life and immortality to light through the gospel. (2 Timothy 1:9–10)

> But when the goodness and loving kindness of God our Savior appeared, He saved us, not because of works done by us in righteousness, but according to His own mercy, by the washing of regeneration and renewal of the Holy Spirit. (Titus 3:4–5)

> Grace to you and peace from God our Father and the Lord Jesus Christ. I thank my God always when I remember you in my prayers, because I hear of your love and of the faith that you have toward the Lord Jesus and all the saints. (Philemon 3–5)

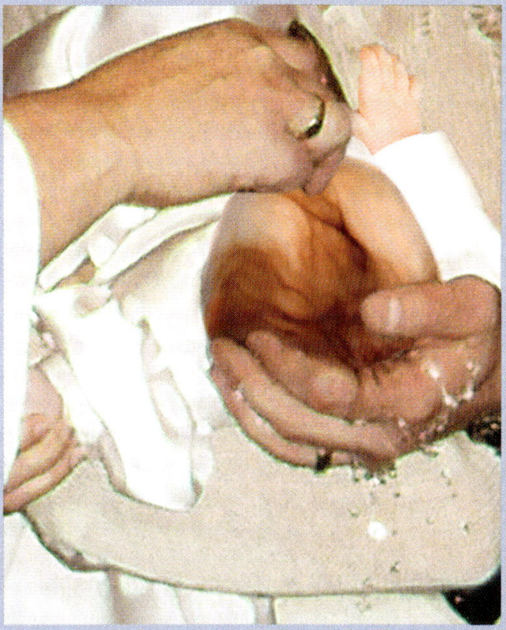

Rejoice!

Whether you serve in an official church position or not, you may feel the pressure of the world and the weight of the Law. Looking to your own deeds and accomplishments, you may believe that you do not deserve such trouble. After all you have done for others, after all you have done for the Lord, God should give you only the best! The Scriptures are clear: "We have all become like one who is unclean, and all our righteous deeds are like a polluted garment. We all fade like a leaf, and our iniquities, like the wind, take us away" (Isaiah 64:6). God saves us not because of what we do, even for Him (Titus 3:4–5).

But God saves you in Christ! Just as he did Timothy, Titus, and Philemon many years ago. Today, Paul writes to you and reinforces the central message of Scripture: God saves you in Christ. Through Jesus, who perfectly obeyed God's Law for you, took your sins and died for you, and rose again for you, God has saved you! "Christ Jesus came into the world to save sinners" (1 Timothy 1:15). God earnestly wants all people to come into a right relationship with Him (2:3–4) through the world's only Mediator, Jesus Christ (v. 5). To that end He has given you the gift of faith, so that you "have [your] hope set on the living God, who is the Savior of all people, especially of those who believe" (4:10). Regardless of how or when you serve the Lord, how much the world dishes out, or even if you undergo the Lord's discipline (Proverbs 3:12; Hebrews 12:11), you can rejoice. God saves you in Christ!

© GARY GLADSTONE/CORBIS

LAW FOR THE LAWLESS

At times, communities enforce some rather strange laws. An edition of *Campus Life* listed some strange obsolete laws still on the books in 1973. For example, in Waterloo, Nebraska, barbers could not eat onions between 7:00 a.m. and 7:00 p.m. It was illegal to use tomatoes as an ingredient for clam chowder in Massachusetts. Men had to ensure that their trousers and jackets matched before going outdoors in Carmel, New York. And you couldn't eat snakes on Sunday, or rattlesnake meat in public, in the state of Kansas. These laws appear ridiculous. How remarkable that punishments were enacted and fines (or jail time!) were imposed. Yet, law-abiding citizens had little reason to fear because laws were not meant for the innocent, but for the guilty!

Christians know that they are forgiven and accepted by God through faith in Christ. They also know that God's Law instructs them in holy living, and that it restrains evildoers and their evil works. But while those things are true, these are not the only uses of God's Law. Paul's First Letter to Timothy tells Christians that God's Law does have a primary use, or purpose. The Law is not only a guide or a curb. Instead, like a mirror reflecting our sins, God's Law also confronts us with our sins. Indeed, God gave His Law for the lawless.

We know that the law is good, if one uses it lawfully, understanding this, that the law is not laid down for the just but for the lawless and disobedient, for the ungodly and sinners, for the unholy and profane, for those who strike their fathers and mothers, for murderers, the sexually immoral, men who practice homosexuality, enslavers, liars, perjurers, and whatever else is contrary to sound doctrine, in accordance with the glorious gospel of the blessed God with which I have been entrusted. (1 Timothy 1:8–11)

The Use of the Law

We can understand why barbers eating onions during shop hours would be objectionable and why folks in Massachusetts would want only white clam chowder. More difficult to comprehend are laws requiring matching suits and those regulating the eating of snake meat. Whether or not we understand the background of these laws, they were enacted for what someone thought was a good reason. Laws should be established to maintain order and to keep the peace. They are ratified to protect the innocent and to punish the guilty.

God's Law does these things and more. Insofar as Christians are sinners and saints at the same time, they still need the Law to illumine their way. So God's Law instructs Christians what to do or refrain from doing (Psalm 119:105). Further, the world would be a dangerous place if laws did not restrain outward evil deeds and keep the peace. Thus, God's Law written on human hearts at creation helps to preserve order in the world (Romans 2:14–15). However, there is another use of God's Law. Paul wrote to Timothy:

Paul originally wrote these words to Timothy because at that time some Jewish believers at the church in Ephesus insisted that Gentile Christians follow God's Law perfectly in order to remain Christian. These misguided believers taught fanciful (and made-up) religious stories and promoted discussions about endless genealogical points. They set themselves up as teachers of the Law, insisting that their followers resist Paul's Gospel of God's grace alone.

That Gospel declares that God sent Jesus into the world to be our sinless Sacrifice, suffering for us on the cross (see 1 John 1:7; 3:5; 2 Corinthians 5:21). But there is more. In sending His Son, "born of woman, born under the law . . . that we might receive adoption as sons" (Galatians 4:4–5), God fulfilled the righteous requirements of His own Law (Matthew 5:17). In the person of Jesus of Nazareth, the Son of God became the Son of Mary, the perfect human being God the Father had desired from the very beginning (1 Corinthians 15:21–23).

In Jesus, our right standing with God—our righteousness—has been settled (Romans 5:19). Thus, for Paul, the claim by some "persons" in Ephesus that believers must also follow the Law to be saved was "vain discussion" (1 Timothy 1:6). By denying the Gospel of Christ's complete fulfillment of the Law, they placed themselves under the Law's condemnation (1:10b–11).

Using the Law Today

We can wrongly believe that, when it comes to our relationship with God, Christ's "job" was to suffer and die for our sins, and our "job" as believers is to follow God's rules in the Bible. When we think this, we begin to substitute our righteousness for Christ's righteousness and deny the Law's primary purpose—to show us our sins. Like the false teachers in Ephesus, we do not understand "what [we] are saying or the things about which [we] make confident assertions" (1 Timothy 1:7). We need to hear Paul's clear words to the Galatian Christians: "All who rely on works of the law are under a curse; for it is written, 'Cursed be everyone who does not abide by all things written in the Book of the Law, and do them' " (Galatians 3:10). By "living" under the Law and justifying ourselves before God, we ourselves become lawless.

The Bible teaches that Christ came not only to *die* for us, but also to live a God-pleasing *life* for us. God accepts us for Christ's sake through the gift of faith, which trusts in His suffering and death *and* in His perfect obedience to God's Law. "Now that faith has come, we are no longer under a guardian," Paul reminds us in Galatians 3:25. Because Jesus has satisfied all of God's requirements, we are able to enjoy all that God has given us through the gift of faith. This is His work in the heart of every believer (1 Timothy 1:5). This gives us a reason to rejoice. The Bible is not simply a "rule book" for living, but truly is the "Good Book," pointing us to Christ. The Law condemns; the Gospel saves. In Christ we are innocent, because God's Law is for the lawless!

God's

Desire in Prayer

One generation shall commend Your works to another . . . They shall speak of the glory of Your kingdom . . . Your kingdom is an everlasting kingdom, and Your dominion endures throughout all generations.
Psalm 145

Much has been made about the "power" of prayer. For example, in *Power through Prayer,* Edward M. Bounds (1835–1913) suggested that personal holiness was the power behind prayer. Recent scientific studies also suggest that patients fare better after surgery, and have shorter hospital stays, if someone is praying for them. Some Christians believe God gives those who pray an ability to assist others or to influence certain events. Because prayer is "powerful," people desire to pray for others and have others pray for them. But what is God's desire behind our prayer?

Paul addresses the subject of prayer in his First Letter to Timothy. He encourages prayer and asks the church in Ephesus to be engaged in prayer. But in contrast to what some people today expect from prayer, Paul puts the focus on God and what He desires through our prayers. God wants us to pray because He desires the salvation of all people.

Praying Together

Not only are we to "call on the name of the Lord" (Psalm 116:13, 17) individually, but also when we as "two or three" (Matthew 18:20) come together in Christ's name. Paul describes prayer in the context of public worship. He emphasizes the important place prayer should have when believers come together to hear God's Word and receive His Sacraments. Men in the congregation should take a leadership position in this regard (1 Timothy 2:8). Calling upon our gracious God is a holy privilege of those who have been redeemed by Christ.

> I urge that supplications, prayers, intercessions, and thanksgivings be made for all people, for kings and all who are in high positions, that we may lead a peaceful and quiet life, godly and dignified in every way. This is good, and it is pleasing in the sight of God our Savior, who desires all people to be saved and to come to the knowledge of the truth. (1 Timothy 2:1–4)

In these verses, Paul offers a summary of prayer in the life of the worshiping community. Prayer's importance cannot be underestimated. Paul strongly encourages Timothy, and through him the church at Ephesus, to be in prayer. The prayers they offer together run the whole gamut of conversing with God: "supplications," or asking God to meet our needs; "prayers," or respectful devotion; "intercession," or earnest appeal to our heavenly Father; and "thanksgivings," which arise from a heart transformed by God's love (Psalm 107:1).

Prayers should be made "for all people," but here Paul emphasizes especially those who exercise authority over us. Despite our attitudes and feelings toward those who hold power, even if they are dishonest, cruel, or incapable, we are to pray for them, even obey them! (Titus 3:1). Our ability to worship and to evangelize as a corporate body, and our potential for exercising our callings as individuals, are hampered by lawlessness and civil unrest. The purpose for such prayers is so that governments and public officials may provide a peaceful and secure society so that the church can flourish.

With Boldness and Confidence

Our prayers, made in faith, please "God our Savior." He wants us to come to Him, as Luther wrote, with "all boldness and confidence . . . [and] ask Him as dear children ask their dear father." The whole of our prayers, and the rich variety of forms they take, are like the smell of sweet incense ascending to heaven (Psalm 141:2). With thankfulness, we are to offer prayers concerning all kinds of temporal things (1 Timothy 4:4–5). However, we do not pray to manipulate, coerce, or intimidate God into doing our will. Rather, we pray as our Lord taught, "Your kingdom come, Your will be done, on earth as it is in heaven" (Matthew 6:10).

God desires the enlargement of His heavenly kingdom of grace by the work of the Holy Spirit through His Word. Just as we do not discriminate in our prayers but pray for "all people," so, too, does God desire the salvation of all people (Ezekiel 18:23, 32; John 3:16). In fact, Paul argues that God is pleased when we pray for everyone because He wants "all people to be saved and to come to the knowledge of the truth" (1 Timothy 2:4). Hence the focus of prayer is not on the required amount of holiness, or the success rate prayer has for the ill, or even the supposed power people have in changing others or altering events. Prayer, whether congregational or individual, is a variety of supplications made in faith to a gracious God. He longs for our prayers, even as He longs to bring salvation to the world.

Our Focus in Prayer

Too often we view prayer in a way that focuses merely on ourselves. We can begin to believe that we're responsible for the outcome of our prayers, that it somehow is related to our "power." Instead of viewing prayer as a humble appeal to an almighty God, we wrongly assume we can control Him by what, how long, or how often we pray. Prayer becomes a tool for getting what we want. With such wicked desires, God may choose not to listen to our prayers at all (Isaiah 1:15). We can hinder our prayers by our misdeeds (1 Peter 3:7).

> The saying is trustworthy, for: If we have died with Him, we will also live with Him; if we endure, we will also reign with Him; if we deny Him, He also will deny us; if we are faithless, He remains faithful—for He cannot deny Himself. (2 Timothy 2:11–13)

In spite of our self-centeredness in our prayers, God's grace still stands. On the cross Jesus prayed, "Father, forgive them, for they know not what they do" (Luke 23:34). Because of Jesus' sacrifice, we know that we are forgiven and that God invites us to come to Him in prayer (John 14:13–14). We can rejoice that He answers our prayers according to His will (Psalm 34:15, 17).

God's Concern for His People

© COMSTOCK.COM

Qualifications for most jobs are rigorous. For example, registered nurses usually possess an associate's or bachelor's degree, have several years of practical experience, and are of good moral character. Certified public accountants generally must earn a bachelor's degree, pass a rigorous CPA exam, and perform their duties ethically. Master electricians are usually required to spend four to five years in an apprenticeship program, pass an exam on the National Electric Code, and be responsible for their work.

Every job or profession requires performance and character. The purpose of these requirements is not to exclude individuals from service. Rather, rigorous qualifications ensure that those who are served—patient, client, and customer—are served well. In the same way, God has established qualifications for those who aspire to the office of the holy ministry. Not everyone will meet these requirements. However, the requirements for the pastoral office are strict, because God is concerned for His people.

More Than Desire

Paul speaks of men who aspire to serve in the pastoral office (1 Timothy 3:1). In the Greek language he's saying that they have a "strong desire." In the same way, laypeople may possess a "strong desire" to serve the church in a particular capacity (altar guild chairperson, choir member, or church officer). But desire alone, apart from any other requirement, does not qualify one for service. Hospitals, professional boards, and trade brotherhoods do not hire, nor do they certify, based on the applicant's wishes. Rather, they ensure that those who wish to serve in these jobs or professions are capable. Positions of service require that the person desiring the job meet the job qualifications and is fit for office.

God Himself has established the qualifications for those who might serve as pastors. Through interviews, schooling, on-the-job training, and professional observations and critique, the church acts as His agent in determining whether a man meets God's criteria for pastor. A pastor, in his position of service, should be fit for office. In a similar way, each congregation should encourage, train, and select people to serve in other needed roles. Desire alone does not make a pastor.

More Than Personality or Ability

Paul lists the qualifications for the public ministry in 1 Timothy 3:1–7 and Titus 1:6–9. At first glance these criteria for serving God's people might look like a profile of personality characteristics. But they are much more than that. In fact, men with a wide variety of personality traits could possibly hold the office of pastor. Some pastors are very outgoing; others are somewhat "bookish." Some pastors are naturally humorous; others have to work at being funny. Some pastors work well with children or teens; others excel with older adults. Regardless of their personality, pastors should meet the qualifications Paul mentions.

Likewise, pastors may possess special abilities in addition to the qualifications listed in the Bible. For example, some pastors are very good at providing leadership at meetings, while others have a special knack for financial details. Some pastors sing or chant excep-

tionally well; others may excel in public speaking or writing. Some pastors may be artistically inclined, while others may be key players in the church golf league. But Paul does not list special abilities one needs to serve as pastor. The ability to do a certain job does not, by itself, qualify one to do it. No matter what special abilities pastors possess, they should meet the qualifications Paul describes.

A Concern for Character

If men are not qualified to serve God's people based on desire alone or by having certain personality types or by exhibiting specific abilities, what are God's qualifications for pastors? Looking again carefully at the lists Paul provides in 1 Timothy and Titus, we can say that the qualifications God looks for primarily concern a man's character. Why is that so? Why is it important for a pastor to be "blameless" or "self-controlled"? Because pastors serve special people: God's people, the church. God gives pastors to His people as a gift (1 Corinthians 12:27–31; Ephesians 4:11–13). Because pastors are God's gift to us, we hold them in high regard and obey their teaching of the Word (1 Thessalonians 5:12–13; Hebrews 13:17).

Certainly we can remember where a pastor or pastors did not exhibit, at all times, all of the qualifications given by Paul. Pastors are sinners too, saved by grace. They also need to confess their sins and receive absolution. What is helpful to remember is that the character traits Paul writes about are themselves gifts of the Holy Spirit. Through the severity of the Law, the Holy Spirit works in the hearts of pastors to lead them to repentance. Through the mercy of the Gospel, the Spirit conforms them to Christ (Romans 12:2; Ephesians 4:1–8; Philippians 2:5–11). When we notice these godly character traits in our pastors, we can give thanks to God. He has given them as gifts to His servants so that they may serve us in love (Galatians 5:22–25; 1 Timothy 4:14; 2 Timothy 1:6–7).

Service to God's People

We can easily turn the Office of the Holy Ministry into a "job" that certain men "perform" in order to achieve prescribed "goals." Having such a view of the pastor's work degrades his calling by God to serve God's people. But having such a view degrades our work as well. God has called us, the baptized, to works of service as mothers and fathers, teachers and plumbers, students and office assistants. He has given us gifts so that we complete our vocations. Our pastor may not meet all of our expectations. But he may fulfill God's qualifications, and refusing or rejecting his office is a refusal of Christ Himself (Luke 10:16; Romans 10:14–15; 1 Timothy 1:20).

"Every good gift and every perfect gift is from above" (James 1:17). God has given you your pastor as a gift to serve you with His spiritual gifts, so that you may serve others in your relationships, job, and professions. God has given you your pastors to call you to faith in Christ our Savior (Ephesians 4:11–13). Through Word and Sacrament, you can be assured of His love and grace. Through your pastor's ministry, you are "being built up as a spiritual house, to be a holy priesthood, to offer spiritual sacrifices acceptable to God through Jesus Christ" (1 Peter 2:5). When your pastor speaks the Word of Christ, you hear the very voice of your Good Shepherd (John 10:27–28). God's requirements for the pastoral office are not easy, nor should they be. For through God's servant—your pastor—God cares for you.

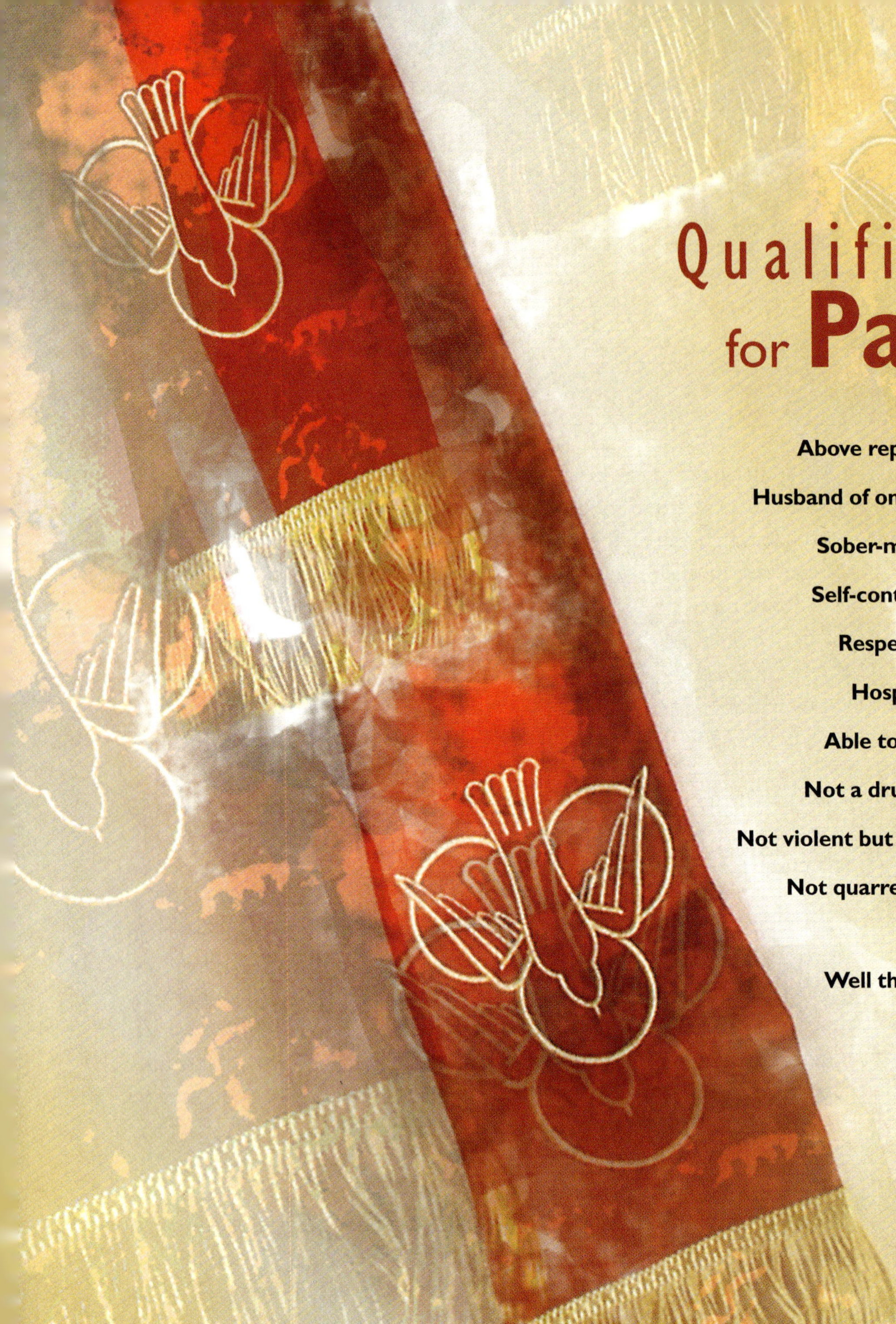

Qualifications for Pastors

Above reproach	I Timothy 3:2; Titus 1:6–7
Husband of one wife	I Timothy 3:2; Titus 1:6
Sober-minded	I Timothy 3:2
Self-controlled	I Timothy 3:2; Titus 1:8
Respectable	I Timothy 3:2
Hospitable	I Timothy 3:2; Titus 1:8
Able to teach	I Timothy 3:2
Not a drunkard	I Timothy 3:3; Titus 1:7
Not violent but gentle	I Timothy 3:3; Titus 1:7
Not quarrelsome	I Timothy 3:3
Well thought of by outsiders	I Timothy 3:7
Not arrogant	Titus 1:7
Not quick-tempered	Titus 1:7
Loves what is good	Titus 1:8
Not a lover of money, not greedy for gain	I Timothy 3:3; Titus 1:7
Manages his own household well, children not insubordinate	I Timothy 3:4–5; Titus 1:6
Not a recent convert	I Timothy 3:6
Upright	Titus 1:8
Holy	Titus 1:8
Disciplined	Titus 1:8
Holds firmly to the trustworthy Word as taught, able to instruct and rebuke according to sound doctrine	Titus 1:9

Study Guide

LifeLight

LifeLight Expands

Available NOW!

LifeLight Original Studies

(available until they are updated to new format; see schedule below)

Isaiah, Pt. 1
Isaiah, Pt. 2
Ephesians/1 & 2 Thessalonians
1 Corinthians
2 Corinthians
Luke, Pt. 1
Luke, Pt. 2
Minor Prophets
Daniel
Life of David
Selected Psalms

LifeLight New Format

(* all-new studies)

1 John
* The Bible: An Overview
Matthew, Pt. 1
Matthew, Pt. 2
* Galatians/Phili/Col
Genesis, Pt. 1
Genesis, Pt. 2
Romans, Pt. 1
Romans, Pt. 2
John, Pt. 1
John, Pt. 2
* 1 & 2 Peter
Exodus, Pt. 1
Exodus, Pt. 2
* James/Jude
Acts, Pt. 1
Acts, Pt. 2
* Proverbs
Hebrews
* Revelation

LifeLight Foundations

Prophecy
Bible Feasts
Miracles

LifeLight Release Schedule

(* all-new LifeLight ** all-new LifeLight Foundations)

2005 RELEASES

**LifeLight Foundations—Law & Gospel — October

2006 RELEASES

LifeLight—Isaiah, Pt. 1 — January
LifeLight—Isaiah, Pt. 2 — April
* LifeLight—Joshua — July
**LifeLight Foundations—Baptism — October

2007 RELEASES

LifeLight—1 Corinthians — January
LifeLight—2 Corinthians — April
* LifeLight—Judges — July
**LifeLight Foundations—Between the Testaments — October

2008 RELEASES

LifeLight—Luke, Pt. 1 — January
LifeLight—Luke, Pt. 2 — April
* LifeLight—Ruth/Esther — July
**LifeLight Foundations—Triune God — October

2009 RELEASES

LifeLight—Minor Prophets — January
LifeLight—Daniel — April
* LifeLight—Mark — July
**LifeLight Foundations—Ministry — October

2010 RELEASES

LifeLight—Life of David — January
LifeLight—Selected Psalms — April
* LifeLight—Ecclesiastes/Song of Songs — July
**LifeLight Foundations—Creation/New Creation — October

<u>Other Future Studies:</u>
1, 2 & 3 John
Job
Wilderness Wanderings (Lev., Num. & Deut.)
Ezra, Nehemiah

<u>These helpful resources are also available:</u>
Intro Kit

To a True Son in the Faith

Distribute before session 1 for use in session 1.
Use Enrichment Magazine pp. 2–4, 8–10 with this session.

1 Timothy 1

Resources for Worship

Use these resources for your daily study at home and at the week's assembly.

Hymn

Chief of sinners though I be,
Jesus shed His blood for me,
Died that I might live on high,
Lives that I might never die.
As the branch is to the vine,
I am His, and He is mine.

O my Savior, help afford
By Your Spirit and Your Word!
When my wayward heart would stray,
Keep me in the narrow way;
Grace in time of need supply
While I live and when I die.

William McComb

Prayer

Almighty God, as You turned the heart of him who persecuted the Church and by his preaching caused the light of the Gospel to shine throughout the world, grant us ever to rejoice in the saving light of Your Gospel and to spread it to the uttermost parts of the earth; through Jesus Christ, Your Son, our Lord, who lives and reigns with You and the Holy Spirit, one God, now and forever. Amen (*LW*, p. 96).

Digging Deep
My Personal Study for Week 1

Day 1 • Read 1 Timothy 1:1–2

1. As with most of the Epistles, this one begins with a salutation, or greeting. In verse 1, Paul not only identifies himself by name, but also by title.

a. What title does Paul claim for himself, and by whose authority did he receive that title?

Acts 1:22

Acts 9:3–6

b. Why would having Paul's credentials in writing be beneficial for Timothy, Paul's co-worker whom he had left at Ephesus, as Timothy carries out his work as outlined in this Letter? Read 1 Timothy 4:11–12.

2. In verse 1, Jesus is described as "our hope."

a. Think about the way you typically use the word *hope* in your daily conversation. Then write out a short definition for this everyday use of the word *hope*.

b. How does the word *hope* take on a different meaning when it is applied to Jesus? In what ways is Jesus *your* hope?

Romans 5:1–5

1 Peter 1:3

c. In what ways is Jesus *your* hope?

3. In verse 2, Timothy is designated as the recipient of the Epistle. With what special phrase does Paul describe Timothy, and what does this indicate about the relationship between these two men? See also 1 Corinthians 4:17.

4. Read Acts 16:1–5. List the things that we learn about Timothy in this passage.

5. As you take one last look at 1 Timothy 1:1–2, note that Paul and Timothy are each named only once.

a. How many times are God and Jesus Christ named?

b. What does the repetition of these divine names imply about the work and ministry to which Paul and Timothy had been called? For help, see 2 Corinthians 3:4–6.

Day 2 • Read 1 Timothy 1:3–7

6. Timothy carried out his work in the city of Ephesus. According to verse 3, what was the chief problem that needed to be addressed there?

7. Why do you think St. Paul addresses *this* issue *first*, before all other issues? That is, why does false doctrine pose such a danger to God's people? See also Galatians 1:6–9.

8. Paul characterizes some of the false doctrine at Ephesus as "myths." Myths are fictional tales or stories. They are not grounded in the truth.

a. List some of the myths that are gaining acceptance in our world today *as if they were true*. (The theory of evolution would be one example.)

b. Why do you think these myths are regarded as truth by so many people in our culture today?

9. According to verse 5, the goal of Paul's command to silence the teachers of false doctrine is love.

a. Read Paul's words in Ephesians 4:1–6. What words or phrases show the loving manner by which false teaching is to be confronted?

b. Now read Ephesians 4:14–16. What results in the church when false teaching is silenced and God's truth is allowed to prevail?

Day 3 • Read 1 Timothy 1:8–11

10. Some of the false teachers at Ephesus were apparently misusing the Law of God—the Ten Commandments (Exodus 20:1–17).

a. What is the main purpose of God's Law in our lives? See Romans 3:20.

b. How do the passages below help us differentiate the Law from the Gospel?

Romans 1:16

Galatians 3:10–11

11. The Law can be used "unlawfully" in the life of the believer. This often happens in one of two ways: Either the Law is overemphasized and predominates over the Gospel, *or* the Law is minimized and ignored.

a. What might be the result in human hearts where the Law predominates and the Good News about Jesus is eclipsed?

Matthew 27:3–5

Living the Faith Together

Distribute before session 2 for use in session 2.
Use Enrichment Magazine pp. 11–13 with this session.

1 Timothy 2–3

Resources for Worship

Use these resources for your daily study at home and at the week's assembly.

Hymn

Lord, open now my heart to hear,
And through Your Word to me draw near;
Preserve that Word in purity
That I Your child and heir may be.

Your Word it is that heals my heart,
That makes me whole in ev'ry part;
Your Word of joy within me sings,
True peace and blessedness it brings.

To God the Father, God the Son,
To God the Spirit, three in one,
Honor and praise forever be
Now and through all eternity!

Johannes Olearius; tr. Henry L. Lettermann

Prayer

O almighty God, by Your Son, our Savior, You have always given to Your Church on earth faithful shepherds to guide and feed Your flock. Therefore we pray, make all pastors diligent to preach Your holy Word and minister Your means of grace, and grant Your people wisdom to follow in the way that leads to life eternal; through our Lord Jesus Christ, who lives and reigns with You and the Holy Spirit, one God, now and forever. Amen (*LW*, p. 104).

Digging Deep
My Personal Study for Week 2

Day 1 • Read 1 Timothy 2:1–7

In chapter 1, Paul commanded Timothy to silence those who were teaching false doctrine. In chapter 2, Paul takes up a new (although not unrelated) topic: worship.

1. In verse 1, Paul uses four synonyms for prayer, each with its own special emphasis. While not unrelated to private, personal prayer, Paul here has in mind the prayers of the church offered as a part of public worship (corporate prayer). Write down some present-day examples of "for kings and all who are in high positions" (v. 2) for whom we might pray. Think both locally and globally!

2. a. It is not too difficult to pray for those authorities who are favorably disposed toward us. However, the leading world authority at the time Paul wrote this Epistle was the Roman emperor Nero, a notorious despot and an enemy of the Christian faith. Why should the church pray for such men? See Romans 13:1–5.

b. What are Christians allowed to do when the governing authority requires us to disobey God and His Word? See Acts 4:18–20; 5:29.

3. a. How many people does God want to be saved (v. 4)?

b. How did Jesus become the "one mediator," the one go-between, "between God and men"?

Verses 5–6

Romans 3:22–25a

c. As you reflect on today's reading, explain in your own words what it means that Jesus is *your* mediator. You might also read Hebrews 9:14–15.

Day 2 • Read 1 Timothy 2:8–15

In these verses Paul now turns his attention to the proper roles of men and women within the context of public worship.

4. In verse 8, Paul expresses his desire that men everywhere should be "lifting holy hands" in prayer.

a. Although prayer can be offered from a variety of postures, what in your opinion is signified by hands lifted upward? (Note how this prayer posture is mentioned in the worship of the Old Testament people of God—Psalm 134:2; 141:2.)

b. What in your opinion is signified by other bodily movement associated with prayer, such as folding hands and kneeling?

5. In verses 9–10, Paul addresses the need for modest and appropriate dress among the women of the congregation. What would be problematic if women were to attend public worship dressed immodestly? (See Colossians 3:1–2.)

6. Read verse 12 together with 1 Corinthians 14:33b–35. As you do so, keep in mind that Paul is addressing the role of women in the public worship of the church. The teaching and speaking which are forbidden to women is the authoritative teaching and speaking done by the pastor. For this reason, only males who are called by the congregation may serve as pastors.

a. Read Galatians 3:28. Did Paul view women as inferior to men?

b. Read 1 Timothy 2:13 and Genesis 2:20. What role was assigned to the woman at her creation?

c. Read Genesis 3:6 and 1 Timothy 2:14. At the time of the fall into sin, did the woman assume a helper or leadership role?

d. What was the consequence given by God to the man for failing to exercise the leadership role God had given him?

Genesis 3:17

Romans 5:12

The Truths of the Faith Must Remain Central

Distribute before session 3 for use in session 3.
Use Enrichment Magazine pp. 17–19 with this session.

1 Timothy 4:1–6:2

Resources for Worship

Use these resources for your daily study at home and at the week's assembly.

Hymn

Lord, keep us steadfast in Your Word;
Curb those who by deceit or sword
Would wrest the kingdom from Your Son
And bring to nought all He has done.

Lord Jesus Christ, Your pow'r make known,
For You are the Lord of lords alone;
Defend Your holy Church that we
May sing Your praise triumphantly.

O Comforter of priceless worth,
Send peace and unity on earth;
Support us in our final strife
And lead us out of death to life.

Martin Luther; tr. Catherine Winkworth, alt.

Prayer

Blessed Lord, since You have caused all Holy Scriptures to be written for our learning, grant that we may so hear them, read, mark, learn and take them to heart that by patience and comfort of Your holy Word we may embrace and ever hold fast the blessed hope of everlasting life; through Jesus Christ, Your Son, our Lord, who lives and reigns with you and the Holy Spirit, one God, now and forever. Amen (*LW*, p. 156).

Digging Deep
My Personal Study for Week 3

Day 1 • Read 1 Timothy 4:1–8

1. Very often when the Scriptures speak of "later times" (v. 1), they are *not* referring only to the days that will immediately precede Christ's second coming. How does Hebrews 1:1–2 help us to understand what is meant by "later times" or "last days"?

2. In verse 1, Paul identifies "deceitful spirits" and "demons" as being responsible for leading some to abandon the faith. However, their faith-destroying work is done indirectly, through false teachers whom Paul describes as insincere "liars."

a. Explain what Paul means when he describes the consciences of such men as having been "seared" with a hot iron. Hint: What is meat like that has been seared?

b. These false teachers were guilty of legalism—of making new laws and demands that the Scriptures do not make. What two examples of legalism are given in verse 3?

3. a. According to 4:4–5, what should accompany our reception of God's good gifts like food and marriage?

b. **Challenge question.** Jesus taught us to pray for "our daily bread" (Matthew 6:11). Why do you think that praying for *daily* bread leads us to receive it with thanksgiving?

4. A more literal translation of Paul's final words in verse 7 might look like this: "Keep on exercising yourself with respect to godliness." List some of the ways that Christians today can get this kind of "exercise."

Day 2 • Read 1 Timothy 4:9–16

5. In verse 10, God is described as "the Savior of all people." We know, of course, that not all people will be saved.

a. In what sense is Jesus the Savior of *all people*?

John 3:16

2 Corinthians 5:19

b. Why will not all people be saved?

Matthew 23:37

Acts 7:51

6. In verse 11, Paul exhorts Timothy to "command and teach" continually the truths of the faith. Why do you think Paul was so insistent about this? That is to say, what will happen in the church when the truths of the faith are *not* continually commanded and taught?

7. **Challenge question.** Since Timothy likely oversaw a number of different congregations, Paul's command to "devote yourself to the public reading of Scripture" (v. 13) probably meant that Timothy was to concern himself with *what sections* were being read, rather than with *doing the reading* himself. Even though all of God's Word is inspired and useful, not all Bible verses are "created equal." Some of the false teachers at Ephesus would have loved to read nothing but the genealogies of the Old Testament (see 1 Timothy 1:4). With this in mind, what do you think makes some sections of Holy Scripture more suitable and edifying for public reading than other sections?

8. Timothy is directed by Paul to keep a "close watch" on both his doctrine and his living. Why must he watch *both* his life *and* his doctrine? What might be the result if only one of these things were watched closely while the other was allowed to go unchecked?

Matthew 7:18

Romans 10:17

Day 3 • Read 1 Timothy 5:1–10

9. In verses 1 and 2, Paul addresses the treatment of people of different sexes and ages.

How are older men to be treated? ________________

Younger men? ________________

Older women? ________________

Younger women? ________________

In a word, Christians are to relate to one another as members of the same ________________.

The Value of Faith above All Other Things

Distribute before session 4 for use in session 4.
Use Enrichment Magazine pp. 20–22 with this session.

1 Timothy 6:3–21

Resources for Worship

Use these resources for your daily study at home and at the week's assembly.

Hymn

A mighty fortress is our God,
A trusty shield and weapon;
He helps us free from ev'ry need
That hath us now o'ertaken.
The old evil foe
Now means deadly woe;
Deep guile and great might
Are his dread arms in fight;
On earth is not his equal.

With might of ours can naught be done,
Soon were our loss effected;
But for us fights the valiant One,
Whom God Himself elected.
Ask ye, Who is this?
Jesus Christ it is,
Of sabaoth Lord,
And there's none other God;
He holds the field forever.

Martin Luther; tr. composite

Prayer

Eternal God and Father of our Lord Jesus Christ, grant us Your Holy Spirit who writes the preached Word into our hearts. May we receive and believe it and be cheered and comforted by it in eternity. Glorify Your Word in our hearts and make it so bright and warm that we may find pleasure in it, through Your holy inspiration think what is right, and by Your power fulfill the Word, for the sake of Jesus Christ, Your Son, our Lord. Amen (Martin Luther).

Digging Deep
My Personal Study for Week 4

Day 1 • Read 1 Timothy 6:3–5

In today's reading Paul again returns to the main point of the entire Epistle: dealing with teachers of false doctrines.

1. In verse 3, "sound words" could be literally translated as "healthy words."

a. Think for a moment of what we mean when we speak of what is healthy and unhealthy in our world today. Why do you think Paul describes true doctrine as "healthy"?

b. Conversely, why could we aptly describe false doctrine as "unhealthy" and "diseased"?

2. The "healthy words" to which Paul refers are the words of our Lord Jesus Christ. Read the following passages and write down what they tell us about the words of Jesus.

Matthew 7:24–27

John 12:48

John 17:14, 17

3. a. In 1 Timothy 6:4, how does Paul characterize the one who teaches false doctrine?

b. What are the effects of such false teaching?

c. How can we avoid being sucked into false teaching? See Acts 17:11.

4. Very often in our world, those faithful Christians who contend for pure doctrine and sound instruction are accused of being divisive and contentious. Reread verses 3–5 together with Romans 16:17–18. According to these passages, who are the real authors of division and controversy in the church today?

Day 2 • Read 1 Timothy 6:6–10

Paul concluded his thoughts concerning false teachers in yesterday's reading by noting that their "godliness" was only a means for financial gain. In today's reading Paul provides some sound instruction concerning the role of money and possessions in the life of the believer.

5. a. How would you define *contentment*?

b. Is contentment (as you have defined it) easy or difficult to achieve? Why or why not?

6. What is the "secret" by which the Christian can find true contentment?

Philippians 4:6–7

Philippians 4:11–13

Hebrews 13:5

7. Does being content mean that Christians are forbidden to set their sights on "better things" than they presently enjoy? Why or why not? (In addition to today's reading, you might reread 1 Timothy 4:4.)

8. Explain the difference between contentment and complacency.

Colossians 3:17

Ephesians 6:7–8

9. If godliness with contentment produces great gain, what is produced by the love of money (1 Timothy 6:9)?

Faith in the Midst of Hardship

Distribute before session 5 for use in session 5.
Use Enrichment Magazine pp. 23–27 with this session.

2 Timothy 1:1–2:13

Resources for Worship

Use these resources for your daily study at home and at the week's assembly.

Hymn

Abide with us, our Savior,
Nor let Your mercy cease;
From Satan's might defend us,
And give our hearts Your peace.

Abide among us always,
O Lord, our faithful friend,
And take us to Your mansions
When time and world shall end.

Josua Stegmann; tr. composite, alt.

Prayer

Lord God, You have called Your servants to ventures of which we cannot see the ending, by paths as yet untrodden, through perils unknown. Give us faith to go out with good courage, not knowing where we go but only that Your hand is leading us and Your love supporting us; through Jesus Christ, our Lord. Amen (*LW*, p. 262).

Digging Deep
My Personal Study for Week 5

Day 1 • Read 2 Timothy 1:1–4

The Book of 2 Timothy is Paul's final Epistle. It could be viewed, in many ways, as the apostle's last will and testament, addressed to Timothy, his dear son in the faith. The words of this Epistle are the words of a dying man, chained like a common criminal (1:16). Yet even under these trying circumstances, the light of the Gospel shines brightly through Paul's inspired words.

1. Here, as in all of his Epistles, Saint Paul was writing under the inspiration of the Holy Spirit. The words he wrote were "breathed out by God" (2 Timothy 3:16). But for the purposes of this question, imagine yourself as Paul. You are chained as a common criminal in a cold dungeon. You are lonely. You know that your earthly life will soon be ending. How might these facts affect the tone and content of your final Epistle to Timothy?

2. a. Even with death staring him in the face, Paul's first sentence refers directly to what promise?

b. What, specifically, does Paul have in mind when he writes of this promise?

2 Timothy 1:10; John 3:16

3. In the face of such dire circumstances and suffering, it is remarkable that Paul begins the body of the Epistle by expressing his thanks to God (v. 3). Think about some of the suffering and trials you have faced in your own life.

a. What thoughts and feelings did you have during one of your trials?

b. After the trial?

c. What did God accomplish in you through the trial?

4. In verse 3, Paul also makes the remarkable claim that his conscience is clear.

a. In your own words, what does it mean to have a clear conscience?

b. Not every dying man has a clear conscience. Why would Paul's conscience have had the potential to be extremely troubled? (Especially prior to his conversion, Paul was also known as Saul.)

Acts 8:1–3; Galatians 1:13

c. What remedy for a guilty conscience is suggested by the following references?

Psalm 32:3, 5; James 5:16

Day 2 • Read 2 Timothy 1:5–12

5. a. According to verse 5, God saw to it that Timothy was raised in the Christian faith. Why should Christian parents take special note of Paul's intergenerational description of the faith?

Ephesians 6:4; Deuteronomy 6:4–9

b. Note again 2 Timothy 1:5 as well as Acts 16:1. What encouragement can be found for single parents and/or parents married to unbelievers?

6. In verse 6, Paul writes of the "gift of God" that Timothy should continue to fan into flame. Read the following passages and from them surmise what special abilities were included in this "gift" that Timothy possessed:

1 Timothy 4:6; 1 Timothy 4:11–14; 1 Timothy 5:17

7. Reading "between the lines" of verse 7, what conclusion might we draw about Timothy's personality? See also 1 Corinthians 16:10–11.

8. In verse 9, Paul writes a beautiful and succinct summary of the Gospel. Answer the following questions using only what is written in verse 9. When it comes to our salvation,

By whom was it accomplished?

Why was it accomplished?

When was it first planned?

9. The verb "abolished" in verse 10 can also be translated as "destroyed," "put out of commission," "annulled," and "rendered inoperative." In your own words, summarize all that it means that Jesus has "destroyed death" and "brought life" to light. See 1 Corinthians 15:51–57.

Day 3 • Read 2 Timothy 1:13–18

10. Many modern readers of Scripture (those who do not accept its authority or inerrancy) take issue with the Epistles of St. Paul. They claim that Paul interject-

Faith Put to Action in Life

Distribute before session 6 for use in session 6.
Use Enrichment Magazine pp. 5–7 with this session.

2 Timothy 2:14–3:17

Resources for Worship

Use these resources for your daily study at home and at the week's assembly.

Hymn

Thy strong word did cleave the darkness;
At Thy speaking it was done.
For created light we thank Thee,
While Thine ordered seasons run.
Alleluia, alleluia!
Praise to Thee who light dost send!
Alleluia, alleluia!
Alleluia without end!

Thy strong Word bespeaks us righteous;
Bright with Thine own holiness,
Glorious now, we press toward glory,
And our lives our hopes confess.
Alleluia, alleluia!
Praise to Thee who light dost send!
Alleluia, alleluia!
Alleluia without end!

From the cross Thy wisdom shining
Breaketh forth in conqu'ring might;
From the cross forever beameth
All Thy bright redeeming light.
Alleluia, alleluia!
Praise to Thee who light dost send!
Alleluia, alleluia!
Alleluia without end!

Martin H. Franzmann, © 1969 CPH

Prayer

O Lord God, bless Your Word wherever it is spoken throughout Your Church. Make it a Word of power and peace to convert those not yet Your own and to confirm those who have come to faith. Let not our foolish and unworthy hearts rob us of the continuing gift of Your precious love, but pardon our sin and complete what You have begun in us. May Your Word pass from the ear to the heart, from the heart to the lip, and from the lip to the life that, as the rain makes the earth to bud and flourish, so also Your Word may achieve the purpose for which You send it; through Jesus Christ, our Lord. Amen (*LW Altar Book*, p. 152).

Digging Deep
My Personal Study for Week 5

Day 1 • Read 2 Timothy 2:14–19

1. By way of review, briefly jot down some of the circumstances under which Paul wrote 2 Timothy. (See session 5, day 1 for help.)

2. a. What is the "word of truth" (v. 15) that Timothy (and we) need to hang on to in order to keep us from quarreling and "irreverent babble"? See Ephesians 1:13.

b. Read ahead to 2 Timothy 4:3. What contrast can be drawn between faithful preachers of the Word, such as Timothy, and teachers of false doctrine?

3. In verse 17, false doctrine is compared to gangrene. The word translated as gangrene could also be translated as "cancer." This is a striking comparison even in our day, as cancer remains a terribly prevalent disease. As you think about this disease and its awful effects, expand on Paul's comparison with false doctrine. Write down as many similarities as you are able to note between cancer and false doctrine.

4. a. Apparently Hymenaeus and Philetus taught that a believer's resurrection was only something "spiritual" and "symbolic," an "awakening" that the believer experienced in conjunction with Baptism and conversion. How does Paul refute this false teaching concerning the resurrection in 1 Corinthians 15:12–20?

b. What effect was Hymenaeus and Philetus's false teaching having? See 2 Timothy 2:17–18.

Day 2 • Read 2 Timothy 2:20–26

In verses 20–21, Paul compares the teachers and members of the visible church to the utensils of a large house. Some of these utensils are "for honorable use," others "for dishonorable." Hymenaeus and Philetus would be examples of wooden and clay utensils, who pursued ignoble purposes by their false teaching.

5. Paul's comparison to household utensils is intended to exhort faithful Christians (utensils for noble purposes) not to be contaminated by those who may claim some affiliation with the church but who are in fact pursuing ignoble purposes (such as Hymenaeus and Philetus). What do the following passages tell us about how we can "cleanse" ourselves of those who pursue dishonorable purposes in the visible church?

a. John 8:31–32

b. John 15:5

c. Romans 16:17–18

d. 1 John 4:1–3

6. "The Lord's servant" of verse 24 refers especially to the called ministers of the church but could also refer to lay people within the church. Such a one, writes Paul, must be "kind to everyone." The word *kind* could also be translated as "gentle." Think about Christians you have personally known who could be described as "gentle." What is the value of gentleness for servants of the Lord

a. in the home?

b. in the congregation?

c. in the work of evangelism?

Day 3 • Read 2 Timothy 3:1–9

7. Recall from an earlier session what Paul meant when he wrote of the "last days," as here in verse 1. He is not referring to the days immediately preceding Christ's second coming; rather, he is referring to . . . (See Hebrews 1:1–2 and 1 Peter 1:19–21 if you need help completing the sentence.)

Guard against Those Things That Attack Faith

Distribute before session 7 for use in session 7.
Use Enrichment Magazine pp. 14–16 with this session.

2 Timothy 4; Titus 1

Resources for Worship

Use these resources for your daily study at home and at the week's assembly.

Hymn

For all the saints who from their labors rest,
All who by faith before the world confessed,
Your name, O Jesus, be forever blest.
Alleluia! Alleluia!

You were their rock, their fortress, and their might;
You, Lord, their captain in the well-fought fight;
You, in the darkness drear, their one true light.
Alleluia! Alleluia!

Oh, may Your soldiers, faithful, true, and bold,
Fight as the saints who nobly fought of old
And win with them the victor's crown of gold.
Alleluia! Alleluia!

The golden evening brightens in the west;
Soon, soon to faithful warriors comes their rest.
Sweet is the calm of paradise the blest.
Alleluia! Alleluia!

William W. How

Prayer

Almighty God, in whose glorious presence live all who depart in the Lord and before whom all the souls of the faithful who are delivered of the burden of the flesh are in joy and felicity, we give You hearty thanks for Your loving-kindness to all Your servants who have finished their course in faith and now rest from their labors, and we humbly implore Your mercy that we, together with all who have departed in the saving faith, may have our perfect consummation and bliss, in both body and soul, in Your eternal and everlasting glory; through Jesus Christ, our Lord, who lives and reigns with You and the Holy Spirit, one God, now and forever. Amen (*LW*, p. 105).

Digging Deep
My Personal Study for Week 7

Day 1 • Read 2 Timothy 4:1–8

Our previous session concluded on a note of high praise for God's gift of the holy Scriptures. They are God-breathed. They are useful. They thoroughly equip us for every good work. Yet it is not enough merely to speak "about" the Scriptures. They must be preached, proclaimed, and applied to the lives of God's people. This is the final charge from Paul to Timothy as the Epistle nears its conclusion.

1. Verse 1 of chapter 4 is the prelude for 4:2. It sets the stage and serves as the basis for the charge that follows. Why do you think Paul chose to reference Christ's judgment of the living and the dead (v. 1) before commanding him to "preach the word . . ." (v. 2)? (See Romans 10:13–17.)

2. The Lord's "appearing" is mentioned both in 4:1 and earlier in 1:10. The same word is used in both places, but it denotes two distinct appearances of the Savior.

a. What was the purpose of His first appearing? See 2 Timothy 1:9–10.

b. What will be the purpose of His second appearing? See Matthew 25:31–46.

3. The command of verse 2 translated as "preach" can also mean "proclaim as a herald." A herald is an authorized messenger who proclaims what has been given him by a superior. Working from this definition, how do each of the following passages explain how the preacher should carry out his work as a herald?

a. Acts 20:27

b. Revelation 22:18–19

c. John 5:39–40

4. **Challenge question.** Explain the imagery of verse 6.

Numbers 28:7, 14, 24

Philippians 1:23

Philippians 2:17

5. In verse 8, Paul writes of the "crown of righteousness" that awaits him. For the Greeks this phrase would call to mind a contestant who had successfully completed a race. His award for victory would often have been a crown or wreath.

a. In what way did Paul already possess the perfect righteousness of Christ, even as he wrote this final Epistle? See Romans 3:22.

b. Why was Paul's perfect righteousness not always perfectly expressed in his earthly life? See Romans 7:23.

c. How will the awarding of the crown of righteousness on the Last Day change things for Paul and for every believer? See 2 Peter 3:13.

Day 2 • Read 2 Timothy 4:9–22

In these concluding verses Paul provides a quick update on his situation and on his fellow servants of Christ. Demas had deserted Paul. Crescens, Titus, and Tychicus were laboring for the Gospel in various regions. Paul was alone except for Luke.

6. In verse 13, Paul asks that Timothy would bring his cloak together with his scrolls and parchments. It is likely that among the scrolls and parchments Paul requested were the Scriptures of the Old Testament. Why might Paul have a special desire for the Scriptures as he wrote this Epistle?

7. In 4:6, Paul writes of the likelihood that he will soon die. Yet, in 4:18, he writes of how "the Lord will rescue" him. How then should we understand the "rescue" Paul anticipates—and for which we pray in the Lord's Prayer? See Matthew 6:13b.

8. Christians are often mistreated and, in Paul's case, actively persecuted because of the faith they confess. The urge to seek revenge—to pay back those who have wronged us—is often a strong desire. How do Paul's words concerning Alexander in verse 14 help us when we get the urge to seek revenge? See also Romans 12:17–21.

Faithful Teaching Produces Faithful Living

Distribute before session 8 for use in session 8.
Use Enrichment Magazine pp. 28–30 with this session.

Titus 2–3

Resources for Worship

Use these resources for your daily study at home and at the week's assembly.

Hymn

Renew me, O eternal Light,
And let my heart and soul be bright,
Illumined with the light of grace
That issues from Your holy face.

Remove the pow'r of sin from me
And cleanse all my impurity
That I may have the strength and will
Temptations of the flesh to still.

Create in me a new heart, Lord,
That gladly I obey Your Word.
Let what You will be my desire,
And with new life my soul inspire.

Grant that I only You may love
And seek those things which are above
Till I behold You face to face,
O Light eternal, through Your grace.

Johann F. Ruopp

Prayer

O my God, though I am a sinner, yet I am not a sinner. On my own and apart from Christ, I am a sinner. But in my Lord Jesus Christ and apart from me, I am no sinner. I firmly believe that He has destroyed all my sins with His precious blood. To show this, I am baptized, cleansed by God's Word, and declared absolved and freed from all my sins. In the Sacrament of the true body and blood of my Lord Jesus Christ I have received the forgiveness of sins as a sure sign of grace. This He has merited, won, and accomplished for me by the shedding of His precious blood. For this I thank Him in eternity. Amen (Martin Luther).

Digging Deep
My Personal Study for Week 8

Day 1 • Read Titus 2:1–10

1. Please answer these review questions drawn from the previous session.

a. Who was Titus, and what do we know about him?

b. Where was Titus serving at the time this Epistle was written, and what was the reputation of the people in that place?

2. The following list of Cretan qualities is taken from 1:12. Reread the list of qualities in Titus 2:2 that Paul commanded be taught to the older men of Crete. For each of the undesirable qualities below, pick the godly quality from verse 2 that stands in sharpest contrast to the natural Cretan characteristics.

Liars

____

Evil beasts

____

Lazy gluttons

____

3. The topic of wine drinking has come up several times in the Pastoral Epistles (1 Timothy 3:3, 8; 5:23; Titus 1:7; and now 2:3). Wine was a plentiful and safe beverage in the first century, where often the water supply was polluted. Wine has some beneficial health effects and can be "received with thanksgiving" (1 Timothy 4:4). However, "much wine" (drunkenness) is not only physically harmful, but spiritually harmful. List some of the ways that drunkenness can be spiritually harmful. (For help with your answer, consider how too much wine might affect the godly qualities of verse 2.)

4. Modern educational theory separates and segregates learners by age. Children learn together with other children. Teens learn with teens. We all learn so much from our peers.

a. What's different about the learning method proposed by Paul in verses 3–5?

b. How have you learned and benefited from a Christian of an older generation?

5. In verse 5, Paul writes that younger women can learn from older women to be "submissive to their own husbands." The apostle gives a fuller explanation of this phrase in Ephesians 5:22–24. Read that passage and complete the following sentence:

The relationship between a husband and his wife should be like the relationship between

________________ and His __________________.

6. When God's people live holy lives according to Paul's directions in today's reading, what is the benefit for outreach and evangelism? See verse 10b.

Day 2 • Read Titus 2:11–15

Yesterday's reading concluded with a reference to "the doctrine of God our Savior" (v. 10). Today's reading shows the effect that teaching has in the lives of believers.

7. a. What is it that motivates and teaches the Christian to say no to ungodliness? In other words, what prompts the Christian to do good works and live a holy life? See also Ephesians 2:8–10.

b. What might have prompted Paul to stress the moral effects of God's grace in this Epistle addressed to Titus in Crete? (See 1:12.)

c. *For personal reflection only.* What worldly passion or ungodliness in your life is the grace of God leading you to say no to? Reflect on that wonderful grace of God now—His forgiving love for you in Christ—and breathe a prayer to God your Father, asking Him to strengthen you to say no in the power of His Spirit.

8. Many Christians are tempted to excuse away sinful behaviors or lifestyles with statements such as "The devil made me do it" or "This is just the way God made me." With such statements they attempt to evade responsibility for their own actions. How might you use Paul's concepts both to confront (Law) and to comfort (Gospel) a fellow Christian who makes such an excuse?

Titus 2:11–14

Romans 6:1–14

Love for Neighbor Arises from Faith

Distribute before session 9 for use in session 9.
Use Enrichment Magazine pp. 31–32 with this session.

Philemon

Resources for Worship

Use these resources for your daily study at home and at the week's assembly.

Hymn

Son of God, eternal Savior,
Source of life and truth and grace,
Word made flesh, whose birth among us
Hallows all our human race,
You our head, who, throned in glory,
For your own will ever plead:
Fill us with your love and pity,
Heal our wrongs, and help our need.

Son of God, eternal Savior,
Source of life and truth and grace
Word made flesh, whose birth among us
Hallows all our human race:
By your praying, by your willing
That your people should be one,
Grant, oh, grant our hope's fruition:
Here on earth your will be done.

Somerset T. C. Lowry

Prayer

Almighty and everlasting God, because You hate nothing You have made and forgive the sins of all who are penitent, create in us new and contrite hearts that we, worthily repenting our sins and acknowledging our wretchedness, may obtain from You, the God of all mercy, perfect remission and forgiveness; through Jesus Christ, Your Son, our Lord, who lives and reigns with You and the Holy Spirit, one God, now and forever. Amen (*LW*, p. 32).

Digging Deep
My Personal Study for Week 9

Day 1 • Read the entire Epistle, noting especially verses 1–3

1. Paul wrote this Letter to Philemon, a believer in Colosse who was a slave owner. One of his slaves, Onesimus, had run away—punishable by death under Roman law. Through Paul's ministry, Onesimus became a Christian—and now was willing to return to his master. Compare Paul's prescript in verse 1 with other prescripts he wrote (e.g., Romans 1:1; 1 Corinthians 1:1; and 1 Timothy 1:1).

a. What self-designation does Paul omit in his Epistle to Philemon, which he typically includes at the beginning of every Epistle?

b. Given that Paul is essentially writing this Epistle to ask a favor of Philemon, why might he have chosen to omit this self-designation?

2. Philemon, the recipient of this Epistle, is not mentioned in the New Testament outside of this Letter. Onesimus, however, the subject of this Epistle, is mentioned in Paul's Letter to the Colossians. Read Colossians 4:7–9. What do we learn about Onesimus in this passage?

3. Philemon's house served as more than a mere dwelling place.

a. What other use did it have (v. 2)?

b. Based on the usage of his house and his ownership of slaves, what could we infer about Philemon's economic status?

4. "Grace" and "peace" form a characteristic greeting of Paul's. Grace is God's undeserved love and favor for all people.

a. In whom is that grace personified and expressed? (Ephesians 1:6–7)

b. With whom do we now enjoy "peace"?

Romans 5:1

Galatians 3:28

5. Although this Epistle is a personal one, intended primarily for Philemon, Paul also greets others. Commentators believe that Apphia was probably Philemon's wife; Archippus was probably his pastor. The church that met in their Colosse home is also greeted. The runaway slave Onesimus would have been known by all of these people. Given Paul's request concerning Onesimus, how would the members of Philemon's family and church also be affected by his decision?

Day 2 • Read Philemon 4–7

In today's reading, Paul tells how Philemon has prompted his thanksgiving and prayers in the past, in the hope that Philemon will continue to give Paul reason for thanksgiving to God.

6. Paul's thanksgiving and prayer in verses 4–7 is not unrelated to his forthcoming request on behalf of Onesimus. In fact, many of Paul's expressions in these verses are echoed again later in the Epistle.

a. In verse 4, Paul relates that Philemon was remembered by Paul in his prayers. How does Paul figure into Philemon's prayers? See verse 22.

b. In verse 5, Paul highlights the quality of Philemon's love. How does Philemon's love come into play with regard to Paul's request concerning Onesimus. See verse 9.

c. In verse 7, Paul writes that he has received joy and encouragement "because the hearts of the saints have been refreshed through [Philemon]." By agreeing to Paul's request, who else's heart would be "refreshed"? See verse 20.

7. The word translated in verse 6 as "sharing" is the Greek word for "fellowship." "Sharing of your faith," therefore, should probably not be understood as "witnessing." Rather, this verse shows that Philemon has been "active" and energetic in matters of fellowship with the other Christian brethren at Colosse. Rather than being passive, Philemon has actively and energetically expressed his fellowship with the saints. In what ways can Christians today actively express their fellowship with other believers? (For help, see Acts 2:42.)

8. *For personal reflection. Sharing optional.* Paul was filled with thanksgiving, joy, and encouragement because of Philemon's active faith and love. Unlike Paul, we sometimes overlook the wonderful expressions of faith and love from our fellow believers. Who has been a source of thanksgiving, joy, and encouragement for you? Why?

9. Paul addresses Philemon as "brother" in verse 7. What effect do you think this word might have had on Philemon as he read this Epistle for the first time?

Day 3 • Read Philemon 8–14

10. There is an old saying that you can attract more flies with honey than you can with vinegar. Paul, of course, was not writing to attract flies but to persuade Philemon concerning Onesimus. Look again at verses 8–9. Apply the "honey versus vinegar" saying to the two approaches noted by Paul.

a. "Vinegar" approach—

b. "Honey" approach—

11. Paul had written more than a third of the Epistle before ever mentioning the name "Onesimus." Why might Paul have refrained from mentioning the name of Philemon's runaway slave earlier in the Epistle?

12. Onesimus was in good company when Paul described him as "my child."

a. Who else enjoyed this designation?

1 Timothy 1:2

Titus 1:4

b. What must Philemon have thought or felt when he first read this description of his runaway slave?

13. The name Onesimus means "useful." Slaves in the first century were often given such names in the hope that their conduct would match their name.

a. Just for fun, pick a positive adjective that would be an appropriate name for you (e.g., "clever" or "graceful").

b. Now pick an adjective that describes who you are in Christ, as a child of God. The following passages might give you some ideas:

Ephesians 5:25–27; Philippians 1:10; Colossians 3:12

14. Read the following references. What important point is made about good works?

Philemon 14

2 Corinthians 9:7

1 Peter 5:2

Day 4 • Read Philemon 15–25

15. In verse 15, Paul uses the passive verb "was parted" to describe Onesimus's escape to freedom. Onesimus's act of running away was wrong and deliberate. Yet, Paul makes it sound as if this separation was perhaps an act of God Himself.

a. What promise does God give us in Romans 8:28?

b. How did God work for "good" in the case of Philemon and Onesimus?

c. *For personal reflection. Sharing optional.* Through what events in your life has God worked some unexpected, undeserved good?

16. **Challenge question.** Martin Luther wrote concerning this Epistle, "What Christ has done for us with God the Father, that St. Paul does also for Onesimus with Philemon" (Luther's Works, American edition: vol. 35, p. 390, copyright © 1960 by Augsburg Fortress, used by permission of the publisher). Using some of the vocabulary from verses 17–19, explain what Luther meant and why we are all like Onesimus.

Day 5 • Read Colossians 3:22–4:1

Some commentators believe that the Epistle to Philemon and the Epistle to the Colossians were written and delivered at about the same time. (Remember, Philemon lived in Colosse.) Read Colossians 3:22–25 with Onesimus and Philemon in mind.

17. Even though the institution of slavery no longer exists in our culture, Paul's God-inspired rules for slaves also apply to workers today. As we go about the tasks of our vocations, we serve our employers, customers, and family members. What points can you apply from this text to your work?

18. What fact would all Christian masters, employers, and CEOs do well to remember (Colossians 4:1)?

19. Take a moment to reflect on and review what you've learned in this course. Briefly skim over sessions one through nine and the Enrichment Magazine. Then complete the following statements.

In my study of the Pastoral Epistles, I was

a. challenged by . . .

b. comforted by . . .

c. surprised by . . .

9. Verses 11–14 serve as the Epistle reading in many Christian congregations on Christmas Eve. How does this reading tie together the celebration of our Lord's birth with His second coming?

10. Verse 14 is a beautiful summary of the Gospel. Which words or phrases in this verse are most meaningful to you? Why?

Day 3 • Read Titus 3:1–2

Today's brief reading is a wonderful text on Christian citizenship. It guides us both in our relation to rulers and authorities and to our fellow citizens. What a wonderful world it would be if all people approached their civic duties in the manner Paul here prescribes!

11. a. In your own words, what does it mean to "be submissive to" rulers and authorities?

b. List some of the rulers and authorities in your life. See also 1 Peter 2:13–17.

12. a. As citizens of a representative republic, we often find ourselves in the position of being "submissive" and "obedient" to authorities against whom we also express dissent and disagreement. At what point might expressions of disagreement and dissent cross the line to reflect a lack of honor (and thereby break God's commandment to honor parents and all in authority)?

b. At what point are we called to resist and disobey rulers and authorities? See Acts 5:27–29.

13. Being a good citizen requires more than just being obedient and doing what our laws require. What phrase in today's reading suggests doing even more than we are required to do?

14. Earthly citizenship carries many blessings and responsibilities. Yet our earthly citizenship will one day come to an end. As nations rise and fall and as political power shifts and sways, what comforting truth remains unchanged according to Philippians 3:20–21?

Day 4 • Read Titus 3:3–8

15. Verses 4–7 are yet another wonderful expression of pure Gospel. What four qualities of God does Paul use in these verses?

16. The phrase "he saved us" is used twice in the NIV in these verses. The first time it is used to tell us the *reason* we have been saved. What is that reason? What reason is specifically excluded by Paul?

17. The phrase "he saved us" (NIV) is used a second time to express the *means* through which God saves. Paul here calls it a "washing of regeneration and renewal." What is the one and only such "washing" God has given us? See Acts 22:16.

18. As Paul constructed this sentence (in the Greek language), the term "washing" cannot be separated from the terms "regeneration and renewal." Where this "washing" is going on, there you will also inevitably find "regeneration and renewal" going on—carried out by the Holy Spirit. How does each of the following passages express the need of every person for this washing of regeneration?

a. 1 Corinthians 2:14

b. Ephesians 2:1

c. Romans 8:7

Day 5 • Read Titus 3:9–15

19. The Greek word for "divisive" (NIV) in verse 10 is the word from which we derive the English terms *heresy* and *heretic*. In its most literal sense it denotes a person whose teaching is "self-chosen." His "self-chosen" teachings are opposed to the sound doctrine handed down by God through Paul and the other apostles.

a. How does Paul tell Titus to deal with divisive people (false teachers, heretics) in the midst of the church?

b. **Challenge question.** For what reasons do you think Paul prescribes such drastic action? (See 1 Corinthians 5:4–6.)

20. To the same degree that Titus is to refute and shun false teachers (heretics), he is also to support and provide for faithful missionaries such as Zenas and Apollos (v. 13). The verb "speed . . . on their way" literally means "to outfit for a journey." Name some of the ways that we can send missionaries on their way today. That is, how can we support missionaries and the proclamation of the Gospel around the world?

21. With what words of the Lord's Prayer (Matthew 6:9–13) do we regularly ask our heavenly Father to bring many others into His kingdom of grace through the work of missionaries?

9. *For personal reflection. Sharing optional.* At his first and most recent court hearing, Paul had been "deserted" by everyone. Yet he was not alone. He was not without help. "The Lord stood by me and strengthened me" (v. 17). The Christian is never truly alone in times of trouble (Psalm 46:1). Our God has promised never to leave us or forsake us (Hebrews 13:5). Reflect on a time in your life when you felt as if everyone had deserted you. In what ways was the Lord beside you, giving you strength during that time?

Day 3 • Read Titus 1:1–4

It seems likely that the Epistles of 1 Timothy and Titus were written at about the same time. Titus held a position in Crete that was similar in nature to Timothy's position in Ephesus, namely, organizing and developing new congregations. While the mission field in Crete was newer and less developed than in Ephesus, similar themes are sounded for both fields of service.

10. Titus is mentioned a handful of times in the New Testament outside of the Epistle addressed to him. Read the following passages about Titus, writing down any insights about his life and ministry.

a. Galatians 2:1–5

b. 2 Corinthians 7:5–7

c. 2 Timothy 4:10

11. Paul describes himself with two titles in verse 1. The first title is "servant" or, more literally, "slave." What wonderful benefits do we as well as Paul have in our role as "slave" of God? See 1 Peter 2:9–10.

12. Paul secondly describes himself as an "apostle." The apostles were a special and distinct group of men. What special authority was given by Jesus to His apostles in Matthew 10:40 and Luke 10:16?

13. In this opening salutation, Paul expresses the goals of his apostolic work in terms of "faith" and the "knowledge of the truth."

a. Why is knowledge *alone* not sufficient for life with God? See James 2:19.

b. While knowledge is a necessary part of faith, what else is involved in a saving faith? See Romans 10:8–11.

14. In verse 1, Paul uses the phrase "God's elect." Read 1 Peter 1:1–2 and compose a definition for this phrase.

15. Like Timothy, Titus is addressed by Paul as a "true child in a common faith." The adjective *common* does not mean "ordinary." It refers, instead, to something shared. All true Christians share together in the faith. Read Ephesians 4:4–5 and Acts 2:42. What are some of the holy things that are shared between Christians?

Day 4 • Read Titus 1:5–9

16. **Challenge Question.** Paul left Titus behind in Crete to "appoint elders [pastors] in every town" (v. 5). The list of qualifications for elders (pastors) in verses 6–9 is very similar to the list in 1 Timothy 3:2–7. The

Epistle to Titus contains identical qualifications (although sometimes expressed with slightly different words).

a. As you compare the lists in both Epistles, what qualification from 1 Timothy is notably absent in Titus?

b. Given that this qualification is not found in Titus and that no qualifications for deacons are found in Titus, what might this reveal about the length of time the church had been in existence in Titus's Crete versus Timothy's Ephesus?

17. In verse 9, Paul gives two reasons why pastors must "hold firm" to the Gospel message: (1) to encourage with sound doctrine and (2) to rebuke those who oppose it.

a. In our day pastors are sometimes criticized when they rebuke those groups and sects that oppose sound doctrine, especially when this is done in public preaching and teaching. In your opinion, why is this rebuking sometimes viewed negatively?

b. Why do you think that Paul says pastors must both encourage sound doctrine *and* refute what is false? Why not just accentuate the positive and ignore the negative?

Day 5 • Read Titus 1:10–16

In today's reading Paul addresses some of the specific false teachings plaguing the church at Crete.

18. In verse 10, Paul goes out of his way to mention "those of the circumcision party." These men were apparently teaching that circumcision and other parts of the Old Testament ceremonial law were still binding.

a. By insisting that circumcision was necessary for salvation, this group was denying the most important teaching of the Christian faith. What is that teaching?

Romans 3:21–24

Ephesians 2:8–9

b. In the Old Testament, circumcision was the outward sign that showed that the individual stood in a covenant relationship with God. By what special sign is that relationship established among God's New Testament people? See Colossians 2:9–12.

19. In verse 11, Paul directs that the false teachers at Crete "must be silenced." This verb can also be translated as "be muzzled" or "gagged." It is a strong word. In contrast, some of the new Christians at Crete would perhaps have advocated an open dialogue with the circumcision group, thereby giving them a chance to at least be heard. Others might have suggested forming a committee to study the circumcision question further. Why do you think Paul took the unyielding position he did? (Note question 18. a.)

20. The Cretans were commonly "liars, evil beasts, lazy gluttons" (v. 12).

a. Think for a moment about the city and state in which you live. What characteristics are common among your neighbors and fellow citizens? (Like Paul, give a brutally honest assessment!)

b. How might the characteristics you just noted help or hinder the attempts of your congregation to reach the unbelievers in your particular area with the Good News of Jesus Christ?

8. Reread Paul's descriptions of the people of the last days in verses 2–4. Pick out at least three of the descriptive words or phrases in these verses and give an example of how such people are at work in the world today. Consult your favorite source for news if you're stymied for contemporary examples.

9. According to verse 5, what makes these unholy people particularly dangerous is that some among them have a form or appearance of godliness. That is to say, much of their vocabulary sounds "Christian," but, in fact, they are contending for ideas and doctrines which deny the central beliefs of Christianity. They may speak about morality and God in general. They may even appeal to parts of the Bible and to prayer.

a. Identify some of the contemporary cults, organizations, and societies that have a Christian appearance or form.

b. How does Paul recommend dealing with such people (v. 5)?

c. What further counsel does the Bible give to us regarding our attitude and actions with unbelievers?

Matthew 5:13–16

1 Corinthians 5:9–11

10. Faced with a world full of deceit and danger, Christians today could easily become discouraged and distraught. What comfort and reassurance can you draw from the following passages?

a. Matthew 16:18

b. John 16:33

c. 2 Timothy 3:9

Day 4 • Read 2 Timothy 3:10–13

In contrast to the godlessness that characterizes the last days, Paul's life reflected the selfless qualities of a true servant of the Lord (2:24). The listing of these qualities in today's reading is not prideful boasting. It is, rather, a humble acknowledgment of the good things God had worked and accomplished in him.

11. a. Of the nine items listed in verses 10–11, why do you think it is significant that "my teaching" is listed first of all?

b. According to 1 Thessalonians 2:13, what should we understand Paul to mean by "my teaching"?

12. How does Philippians 3:7–11 help us understand what Paul means when he writes of "my aim in life" (v. 10)?

13. In verse 11, Paul draws Timothy's attention specifically to the persecutions he endured at three cities in Timothy's home province of Galatia, including Timothy's hometown of Lystra. What happened to Paul at:

a. Antioch? (See Acts 13:49–51.)

b. Iconium? (See Acts 14:1–7.)

c. Lystra? (See Acts 14:8–20.)

Day 5 • Read 2 Timothy 3:14–17

14. The Greek word *brephos* is translated in verse 15 as "childhood." It is often translated simply as "child" or "infant." In fact, this word is used in Luke 1:41 to describe the unborn John the Baptist, who leaped in his mother's womb.

a. What does Paul's use of this word indicate about how early in a child's life he or she should be taught the Holy Scriptures?

b. Since the inspired writers of the Bible have used the same word (*brephos*) to denote infants as well as babies still in their mothers' wombs, what conclusion might we draw about when human life begins?

15a. What does it mean that all Scripture is "God-breathed" (NIV)? See also 2 Peter 1:21.

b. *Agree or Disagree? Explain why if you disagree:* The Bible contains the Word of God.

16. How does Satan, the "old evil foe," seek to cast doubt on God's Word, the Holy Scriptures? (Note the question found in Genesis 3:1.)

17. The Godbreathed Scriptures make us thoroughly "equipped." In the first century this same Greek word was used to describe wagons or rescue boats that were completely outfitted and fully furnished. Today we might speak of an automobile that is "fully loaded" with options and features. Tell about a time when *you* experienced the power of God through a Scripture passage that comforted you, strengthened you in a time of trial, enabled you to lovingly admonish a brother or sister in Christ, or had some other immediately beneficial effect. Thank your heavenly Father now as you remember that time.

ed his own personal opinions on matters like the role of women and sexuality. Read the following references. How do you think Paul would respond to those who only follow certain portions of his Epistles, while ignoring other portions?

2 Timothy 1:13; 1 Corinthians 14:36–38; 2 Thessalonians 2:15

11. In verse 14, Paul again writes of the good "deposit" with which Timothy was entrusted. Review question 17 of Session 4. Using only a phrase or sentence, describe what this good deposit is.

12. Paul writes that the help of the Holy Spirit is necessary to guard the good deposit. What does each of the following passages tell us about *how* the Holy Spirit helps us guard this good deposit?

a. John 14:26

b. Ephesians 5:18–20

c. Romans 8:26–27

13. a. Given Paul's circumstances as he wrote this Epistle, together with his statement in verse 15, do you think Paul would have been judged to be a "successful" pastor by today's standards of success? Why or why not?

b. By what standard should a pastor's ministry be evaluated? Look ahead to 2 Timothy 4:2–5 as a guide for your answer.

Day 4 • Read 2 Timothy 2:1–7

Paul concluded the previous chapter of this final Epistle by sharing a few details regarding his present situation. In 2:1, however, Paul directs his heartfelt words most especially to Timothy ("my child").

14. a. A literal translation of 2:1 might say, "You, then, my child, continually be made strong by means of the grace that is in Christ Jesus." Timothy's strength would come not from his own inner self, but by the grace of Jesus Christ. How would you define this strength-giving grace?

2 Corinthians 12:9–10; Ephesians 2:4–5

b. *For personal reflection. Sharing optional.* In what ways has the grace of Jesus strengthened you?

15. In verses 3–6, Paul compares Timothy's service as a minister to three different types of people. Reflect on these three comparisons. In what sense would Timothy's service be like that of

a. a soldier?

b. an athlete?

c. a farmer?

16. a. The command of verse 7 ("think over") could also be translated, "Be applying your mind to." In other words, the Scriptures are not only spiritual words aimed at the heart, but words which are also intended to engage our minds! How does this command help you to understand the importance of family devotions, attending public worship, and Bible classes such as *LifeLight*?

b. Note the future tense of the verb in verse 7. As one who studies the Scriptures and applies your mind to them, what comfort could you draw from this future tense verb?

Day 5 • Read 2 Timothy 2:8–13

Verses 8 and 9 in many ways constitute the very heart of this Epistle. As Paul looks ahead to the approaching day of his death, he is inspired by the Holy Spirit to leave these beautiful words as an enduring testimony to Timothy, his son, and to all the saints of God.

17. In verse 8, Paul encourages Timothy to always remember Jesus Christ. Yet he does not stop there. He goes on to clarify and expand on the very identity and work for which Jesus is to be remembered.

a. "Risen from the dead"—His resurrection proclaims His deity. Why was it necessary for Jesus to be true God?

Psalm 49:7–9; Acts 20:28b; 2 Corinthians 5:19

b. "The offspring of David" points to the human nature of Jesus. Why did Jesus have to be true man?

Romans 5:19; Hebrews 2:14–18

18. a. We remember Jesus as true God and true man, the Savior of all. Yet, many people have a view of Jesus that is only partially correct (e.g., "He was a good teacher of moral values"). Write down some of these incorrect or partially correct views of Jesus.

b. Why are partial and incomplete views of Jesus a serious matter?

John 3:36; John 8:24

19. Verses 11–13 may have been an early Christian hymn.

a. The phrase "If we have died with Him" (v. 11) refers to more than just physical death. By what means has every Christian "died" with Christ? See Romans 6:3–4.

b. How does verse 12 speak to the experiences of Paul and the church at his time (as well as ours)? See also Romans 8:18.

20. What lines or phrases of this hymn do you think would be especially important and comforting to Paul and to other Christians who were subject to persecution and death because of their faith in Jesus Christ?

Day 3 • Read 1 Timothy 6:11–16

Having given due warning about the love of money, Paul now positively depicts how true godliness finds expression in the life of every child of God.

10. Paul gives two commands in verse 11. They might literally be translated, "Keep on fleeing" and "Keep on pursuing."

a. "Flee" is a rather strong command. What are some of the things from which people usually flee?

b. From what is Timothy (and every Christian) to keep on fleeing (v. 10)? (Review yesterday's reading for help.)

11. Paul's command to "pursue" could also be translated "hunt." There is an intensity expressed by this word. What, specifically, should we keep on pursuing (v. 11)?

12. In verse 12, Timothy is charged to "Fight the good fight of the faith." "The faith" does not refer to Timothy's own personal saving faith, but to the substance of the entire Christian faith—the sound teaching and pure doctrine God reveals in the Holy Scriptures. With what "weapons" can Christians contend for the faith today? See Ephesians 6:13–18.

13. Although we cannot "see" God (v. 16), we *can* "hear" and "recognize" him in many ways. According to the following passages, where and when can you confidently "see" God at work in your life?

Matthew 18:20

Romans 6:3–4

1 Corinthians 11:23–26

Day 4 • Read 1 Timothy 6:17–19

Earlier in chapter 6, Paul addressed people who "desire to be rich." He now writes concerning the godly Christians who already *are* rich.

14. Write down a three-point summary of Paul's directives for those believers who are rich.

a.

b.

c.

15. a. Verse 17 reminds us that God "provides us with everything to enjoy." Even unbelievers receive earthly blessings from God. What purpose and hope does God have in so richly blessing all people?

Acts 14:11–17

Romans 1:19–20

b. What is the result in the hearts of those who stubbornly refuse to acknowledge and give thanks to God for all that He gives them?

Romans 1:21–25

Ephesians 4:18–19

c. What attitudes and actions in our world today indicate people's denial that it is God who provides all that they have?

16. **Challenge question.** Read the parable of the rich fool in Luke 12:16–21. Given what Paul has said concerning riches in 1 Timothy, and noting especially that they can be a curse or a blessing for our enjoyment, identify the sin(s) of the rich man in this parable.

Day 5 • Read 1 Timothy 6:20–21

Paul's concluding appeal in these two verses serves as a good summary of the entire Epistle.

17. In verse 20, Paul tells Timothy to "guard the deposit entrusted" to him. Paul, of course, is not referring here to money. Review the following passages from 1 Timothy and write down briefly how each one expresses the nature of the "deposit" Timothy is to guard.

1:11

1:15

3:16

4:10

18. Popular culture encourages us to engage those who hold beliefs different from our own—to learn from one another, to find common ground, and to celebrate diversity. Yet Paul commands a different course of action in the case of those engaged in "irreverent babble" and "contradictions."

a. What action is prescribed (v. 20)?

b. For what reason does Paul command such action (v. 21)?

19. *For personal reflection. Sharing optional.* As you reflect on your study of 1 Timothy in these first four sessions, jot down at least two things that you found to be especially encouraging or edifying. Then write down any new insights you gained from your study of 1 Timothy.

10. With verse 3, Paul turns his attention to the care of widows in the church. It seems as though a plan for dealing with the widows had recently been introduced, although perhaps not in all the congregations.

a. Why do you think widows (especially in the first century) would have a special need for assistance from the church?

b. Why were not all widows treated with exactly the same amount of assistance? (Note the qualifying phrase used in vv. 3 and 5.)

11. Children and grandchildren have the primary duty of caring for older family members.

a. Why is the word that Paul uses to describe the care that the aged receive from their children and grandchildren an appropriate word (v. 4)?

b. How does God regard this care?

c. In the Fourth Commandment, God tells us that all parents (including those of advanced years) should be served and honored and loved. Yet someone has said, "One father is able to keep and provide for ten children while ten children often cannot see their way clear to take care of one old father." Why do you think this is often the case today for elderly parents, including widows?

Day 4 • Read 1 Timothy 5:11–16

In today's reading Paul addresses the younger widows who were still of childbearing age. Such young widows would have been far more common in the first century than today.

12. The church at Ephesus apparently maintained a list of widows who were receiving support from the church. What three requirements had to be met for a widow to be added to the list (vv. 9–10)?

13. Why are "gossips and busybodies" (v. 13) especially destructive in the life of the church? (See James 3:3–6.)

14. In your opinion, why are gossiping and slander hard for all of us to combat? (What makes this sin against the Eighth Commandment so attractive?)

15. *For Personal Reflection.* In the Large Catechism, Luther gives this advice: "If you encounter somebody with a worthless tongue who gossips and slanders someone, rebuke him straight to his face and make him blush for shame. Then you will silence many a one who otherwise would bring some poor man into disgrace. . . . For honor and a good name are easily taken away, but not easily restored" (THE BOOK OF CONCORD: THE CONFESSIONS OF THE EVANGELICAL LUTHERAN CHURCH, edited by Theodore G. Tappert, copyright © 1959 Fortress Press. Used by permission of Augsburg Fortress, 401:273).

Whom do you know in the church or among your relatives and friends who continually makes your ears a receptacle for gossip and slander? How might you lovingly help that person to repent? Are you yourself willing to be rebuked by another should you be found guilty of the same sinful talk? Talk to your heavenly Father, asking for His help and guidance.

Day 5 • Read 1 Timothy 5:17–6:2

The remainder of chapter 5 is mostly devoted to the treatment of elders, or what we today would call pastors. ("Overseer," "elder," and "bishop" [used in some translations] should in most cases be understood as "pastor.")

16. Verse 17 speaks of the "honor" due to pastors. Which of the following characteristics makes a pastor worthy of honor? Rank in order, with 1 being the most important all that apply. Add one or more that you believe is important.

_____ a sparkling personality

_____ a good teller of jokes

_____ a good administrator

_____ a sharp dresser

_____ explains God's Word effectively

_____ lovingly accepts all viewpoints

_____ ______________________

17. Explain in your own words the point Paul is making when he quotes Deuteronomy 25:4 and Luke 10:7 in verse 18.

18. What protection is offered to pastors against those who might trump up some charge through ill will or hate (v. 19)?

19. Not all charges against pastors are trumped up, however. In verse 20, Timothy is instructed to rebuke those pastors who have sinned. The sin here described would not be the gravest kind of sinning, such as would preclude a man from continuing to serve as a pastor. Note that the ESV speaks of this rebuke occurring "in the presence of all." This probably meant in front of the other elders/pastors. What would be the benefit of rebuking a sinning pastor in the manner Paul here prescribes?

20. Verses 1–2 of chapter 6 address the relationship between slaves and their masters. Slavery in the first-century Roman world was commonplace. Many slaves were well educated and were not living in want.

a. What does Paul urge of believing slaves? Why?

b. What correlations can be made to employers and employees?

7. Verse 15 presents some challenges for the student of the Bible. The phrase "through childbearing" should certainly not be understood to mean that giving birth to children is the means by which women are saved. A more likely meaning is that childbearing is the typical, natural role and function of the woman who is saved. Bearing in mind what we know about the doctrine of justification from other sections of Scripture (see especially Ephesians 2:8–9), by what means are women (as well as men) saved eternally?

Day 3 • Read 1 Timothy 3:1–7

In chapter 3, Paul stresses the important qualifications for those who would serve as "overseers" and "deacons" in the church. An "overseer" is undoubtedly what we would call a pastor today.

8. How do the qualifications for overseers listed in verses 1–7 relate to Paul's overall concern for sound doctrine set forth in chapter 1? In other words, what is the connection between the service of qualified pastors and purity of doctrine?

9. *Pastor* is the Latin word for "shepherd." How is the work of a pastor similar to the work of a shepherd? (See Acts 20:28–30.)

10. Describe in your own words why the pastor's calling is a "noble" or excellent task (v. 1). (Consider 1 Timothy 1:15, 16.)

11. To be "above reproach" literally means, "not to be taken hold of." If a man is above reproach, then no charges of unfitness leveled against him can take hold. Why is it necessary for pastors to be held to such a high level of conduct? See 1 Peter 5:2–3.

12. **Challenge question.** That the pastor be "husband of one wife" (v. 2) suggests that many candidates for the ministry were coming from a pagan background of polygamy and sexual excess.

a. How does this phrase *implicitly* address any demands that ministers *not* be married?

b. How does this phrase *implicitly* speak to the gender of those who serve as pastors?

Day 4 • Read 1 Timothy 3:8–13

Apart from these verses, the Scriptures give us little specific information about the office of deacon. It is clear that they were not pastors. Deacons often assisted the pastors by caring for the place of worship and by visiting the sick and needy of the congregation. Many lay leaders in modern congregations fill a role similar to that of deacon.

13. Read about the first deacons in Acts 6:1–6. Describe the circumstances that led to their selection.

14. "Double-tongued" (NIV) in verse 8 could be translated as "devious." In your own words, define a double-tongued person and tell why it would be inappropriate for such a one to serve as a leader in the church.

15. Given the nature of the deacons' work as described above, why would it be important that their wives be respectable, temperate, and trustworthy (v. 11)?

16. **Challenge question.** What if a pastor is an "unworthy" person—someone who lives in secret sin and/or is an unrepentant hypocrite? Does that mean that when he preaches about Jesus, baptizes people, or administers Communion, the Word of God is not valid?

Matthew 28:18–20

Philippians 1:16–19

Day 5 • Read 1 Timothy 3:14–16

17. In verse 15, Paul uses three different phrases to describe the church. Please write down each of those three phrases; then tell what special characteristic of the church is illustrated by each phrase.

a.

b.

c.

18. The words of poetry in verse 16 were very likely an early Christian hymn about Jesus. The first line is literally translated, "He was manifested *in the flesh.*" What important doctrinal truth about Jesus do these words accent?

John 1:1, 14

Hebrews 2:14–15

19. In what sense was Jesus "vindicated" by the Spirit (v. 16)?

Romans 1:4

1 Peter 3:18

20. When was Jesus "seen by angels (v. 16)?"

Matthew 28:1–3

Acts 1:9–10

Luke 18:9–12

b. What might happen in human hearts where the Law is minimized or ignored?

12. 1 Timothy 1:9 should not be understood to mean that the Law has no place at all in the lives of the righteous. But rather, the curse of the Law (the Law as a means to become right with God) has been abolished by Jesus Christ.

Challenge Question: In verses 9 and 10, Paul includes a list of sinners who stand condemned under the Law. Compare this list with the Ten Commandments. How many of the Ten Commandments are at least indirectly addressed by this list? (You can find the Ten Commandments listed in Exodus 20:1–17.)

13. Read the following verses, define the "glorious Gospel" (v. 11), and tell why it is "glorious."

Romans 6:23

2 Corinthians 5:20–21

Ephesians 2:8–9

Day 4 • Read 1 Timothy 1:12–17

In today's reading Paul turns to the past experiences of his own life to illustrate the abundant grace of the Lord Jesus Christ.

14. Paul (also known as Saul) had experienced God's grace in a powerful and profound way. The apostle describes himself as having been "a blasphemer, persecutor and insolent opponent." What do the following verses tell us about Saul's sin and its ultimate target?

Acts 7:59–8:3

Acts 9:1–5

15. "The saying is trustworthy." This phrase (or a variant) is not used anywhere else in the New Testament except in the Pastoral Epistles to indicate an important truth. For each of the following passages, write down the important truth denoted.

1 Timothy 1:15

1 Timothy 3:1

1 Timothy 4:9–10

16. Reread the long list of sinners in 1:9–10.

a. How does Paul rate himself in comparison to these and all other sinners (v. 15)?

b. Paul understood that the grace and mercy God poured out in his life were to serve "as an example to those who were to believe" (v. 16). That's you! As you reflect on the sin in your own life, what hope and encouragement do you find in the "example" of Paul's life?

17. In verse 17, Paul concludes his recounting of sin and grace in his own life with a doxology, a concise expression of praise to God. Another doxology can be found in Romans 11:33–36. Take a moment to reflect on all that the triune God has done for you, beginning at your Baptism. Think about all He is still doing for you today, and keep in mind His promises for the

future. Now try your hand at writing your own personal doxology.

Day 5 • Read 1 Timothy 1:18–20

18. When Paul instructs Timothy to "wage the good warfare" he is using military language. This phrase highlights the intense spiritual battles that Timothy and every child of God must fight. According to the following passages, against *whom* are we fighting?

1 Peter 5:8–9

1 John 2:15–17

Romans 7:18–25

19. Some Christians hold the belief "Once saved; always saved." That is, a person can never lose the gift of saving faith. Evaluate this teaching based upon Paul's exact words in verse 19. See also 1 Corinthians 10:1–12. What conclusion do you reach?

20. **Challenge question**. In verse 20, Paul gives a concrete example of the extreme action that must sometimes be taken against unrepentant sinners. Hymenaeus and Alexander are mentioned by Paul as examples of those who have "made shipwreck of their faith" (v. 19). Read 2 Timothy 2:17–18. Although this is a somewhat difficult text to understand, scholars believe that Hymenaeus and Alexander taught that Christians experience only a spiritual resurrection, not a bodily resurrection.

a. Why is it imperative to have a correct understanding of Jesus' and our own bodily resurrections? See 1 Corinthians 15:12–20.

b. What was the result of their false teaching (2 Timothy 2:18)?

21. Church discipline is that process by which the church seeks to deal with openly unrepentant sinners. What attitudes should guide and direct the process of church discipline?

Galatians 6:1–2

Ephesians 4:2–3

22. **Challenge question.** Excommunication is that final step of church discipline taken against those who have rejected the faith by their refusal to repent. An excommunicated person is to be excluded from the rights and privileges of a Christian. This action had apparently been taken against Hymenaeus and Alexander. The purpose of excommunication is never to punish the sinner.

a. What purpose for excommunication is expressed?

1 Corinthians 5:5

1 Timothy 1:20

b. What additional reason for excommunication can be found?

Matthew 18:6

1 Corinthians 5:6?

c. In your opinion what should be done for an excommunicated sinner who repents?

Luke 15:1–7

2 Corinthians 2:7–8.

A new television game show, *Nothing But the Truth*, filmed its pilot episode in 1955. Hosted by Mike Wallace, the show asked five contestants to determine the true identity of Tony (or Toni) Costello, a truant officer. After a series of questions and answers, only one contestant was right. He successfully chose Mr. Tony Costello over two female competitors. Later that year, *Nothing But the Truth* made its television debut as *To Tell the Truth*.

In today's world the concept of truth, as well as the ability to tell it, has taken a beating. Some people no longer believe that truth exists or, if it does, it is true only for those choosing to believe it. Truth is "relative," they say. Such skepticism has caused a lot of concern and worry, particularly concerning religious beliefs. How (if it is at all possible) do we separate truth from error when it comes to our faith? In contrast to the uncertainty and disbelief of our age, Paul offers a powerful corrective regarding truth. He vigorously contends that God gives us reliable, eternal truth in our Savior, Jesus Christ.

Truth Denied

Our modern "truth tangle" has been referred to as postmodernism. Postmodernism places little value on our ability to understand the world around us. Even if we were able to experience or observe certain events or objects, we still would not be able to categorize, analyze, and comprehend them. Without such ability, postmodernism says, we are unable to maintain a comprehensive explanation of anything. Each of us is left to fabricate our own truths, what we feel is personally true for us. In such an environment and with such a belief, how does one tell the truth?

Timothy faced such a challenge in ministering to the church at Ephesus. Ephesus was one of the centers of Rome's Asian province, ranking with Antioch and Alexandria in importance. Most notable in the city was the glorious temple of Artemis (Diana), listed among the seven wonders of the ancient world. The city itself was full of all sorts of religious teachers, each proclaiming his or her version of spiritual truth. The members of Timothy's congregation heard from a variety of people all claiming to tell the truth.

To make matters worse, false teachers trying to sell their own brand of truth had arisen within the Ephesian congregation. These men distorted the true message of God's salvation by His grace through faith in Jesus Christ. They taught that God's undeserved favor on account of Christ was not enough. Good works, that is, following God's Law, were also necessary for salvation, they said. These false teachers promoted not peace but controversies by their teachings (1 Timothy 1:4). Paul warned Timothy that later some teachers would go so far as to advance unsound doctrines they themselves had learned from demons (4:1–3).

Truth Received

Paul believed in objective truth, which transcends one's perceptions, experiences, or opinions. He both encouraged and challenged Timothy to follow his call as the congregation's pastor in sharing the truth of the Gospel of Jesus Christ. Paul knew that God desires that every person be saved and "come to the knowledge of the truth" (1 Timothy 2:4). Other called leaders like Timothy should be faithful to the biblical doctrine, which is truth (3:9; see 2 Timothy 2:15). The church, the body of Christ indwelt by the Holy Spirit, is the foundation and pillar of truth (1 Timothy 3:15). Those teaching false doctrine, conceited and lacking in understanding, often do so for monetary gain, Paul said. Such teachers have been robbed of, or have wandered away from, the truth (6:5; see 2 Timothy 2:18).

Thus objective truth, evidenced by God's grace in and through Jesus Christ, exists. Paul gives further proof of the existence of truth by denouncing "false" teachers. (If Paul did not believe some teachings were "true," he could not argue against others that were "false.") The clear truth of Christ and His salvation is the very reason God called Paul to apostleship: "for the sake of the faith of God's elect and their knowledge of the truth, which accords with godliness, in hope of eternal life, which God, who never lies, promised before the ages began" (Titus 1:1–2). Objective truth, received as God's infallible and never-changing Word (John 10:35; 17:17; 2 Timothy 3:16–17; 2 Peter 1:21), points always to the truth made human flesh, Jesus Christ (John 1:14, 17; 5:39; 14:6).

Truth Transmitted

Paul encourages Timothy to abide by and convey the truthful teachings entrusted to his care. "If you put these things before the brothers," he says, "you will be a good servant of Christ Jesus, being trained in the words of the faith and of the good doctrine that you have followed. . . . Command and teach these things" (1 Timothy 4:6, 11). Pastors should have the capability to, and are specially charged with, teaching biblical truth (1 Timothy 3:2; 5:17; Titus 1:9). Their hearers owe them godly respect and loving obedience (1 Thessalonians 5:12–13; Hebrews 13:17), because of the position of "truth-telling" entrusted to their pastors.

The objective truth claims made by God Himself and recorded in His Word—creation and redemption, sin and grace, Law and Gospel, death and life—are not to be hidden, but are to be taught in faithfulness. The pattern of sound teaching (2 Timothy 1:13–14) taught by Paul is not merely to be carefully preserved, but by the Holy Spirit's power carefully communicated to all who follow, or would follow, Jesus Christ. Paul's antidote for a variety of "truths" in Timothy's congregation was the truth made flesh, written in the truth-filled Scriptures and proclaimed from truth-flowing pulpits. "Declare these things; exhort and rebuke with all authority. Let no one disregard you" (Titus 2:15).

What Is Truth?

We may be like Pilate, who asked Jesus, "What is truth?" (John 18:38). Quite unaware of the influence postmodern culture has had on our own thinking, we may deny part or all of God's objective truth recorded in His Word. We may select passages of Scripture we agree with, while denying the rest. We do this particularly when the Bible confronts and condemns our sinful thoughts, words, or deeds. By not confessing "the truth, the whole truth, and nothing but the truth" when it comes to our sin, we do not "tell the truth." We make God out to be a liar, and we deserve His eternal wrath.

The truth made flesh, Jesus Christ, exists, even for those who deny Him. He came objectively as a baby born in Bethlehem to His virgin mother. In everything He did, He obeyed the Law of His Father. He died a cruel death on a cross for our sins, and he was raised for our justification, releasing us from a sentence of death. "He was manifested in the flesh, vindicated by the Spirit, seen by angels, proclaimed among the nations, believed on in the world, taken up in glory" (1 Timothy 3:16). The truth made flesh speaks His truth through His truth-filled Word. Jesus our Savior will never lie nor deceive. What is truth? Jesus Christ, our Savior, and what a truth to tell! In a skeptical and worried postmodern world, His truth gives us eternal comfort and joy.

For the Love of Money

A new $20 bill made its debut October 9, 2003. Printed with green, peach, and blue ink, this colorful bill possesses a watermark and an interwoven security thread. Released by the U.S. Federal Reserve System under their program "The New Color of Money," it is the first American bill in modern history to exhibit background colors other than green and black. The Federal Reserve hopes the bill's new color scheme will frustrate the efforts of counterfeiters.

Whether old colors or new, the appeal of money can be powerful at times. It will always have a certain attraction. For some, money represents security from the rough-and-tumble of life. For others, it brings greater happiness through the accumulation of pleasurable experiences or material possessions. However, while these claims about money are very alluring, they are really "counterfeit." God's Word shows us that God provides us money to provide for our basic needs.

Money's "Value"

Did you know that paper money has no real value? A single bill, regardless of the denomination printed on it, costs less than five cents to manufacture. It is virtually worthless! The only value paper money has is assigned to it by the U.S. Treasury. Without the backing of our government, the true value of paper money (and coinage) is "nothing." Likewise, any other form of money we have accumulated—real estate, stocks, retirement funds, or personal property—has value only because of our government's support of a regulated currency and a stable financial market.

Our federal government assigns and backs the value of each piece of paper money in circulation. As individuals, we also assign what power, influence, and control money will have in our lives. That is the true value we place on money. Certainly, we are confident God will meet all of our basic needs (Philippians 4:19). But how much do we rely on wealth to shield us from life's ups and downs? How preoccupied are we with preserving what we have or gaining more? Should we desire financial resources providing for much more than food, clothing, and shelter?

The Love of Money

Many people believe that the Bible says, "Money is the root of all evil." Far from it! Money, as part of what God provides, is a blessing. It is His gift given simply by grace through our efforts of work or investment (Luke 10:7; Proverbs 10:4; 14:23; 21:5). We should never worry about having enough money to provide for our basic needs (Luke 12:22–26). However, we should be concerned when our thoughts and devotion center primarily on our financial resources or our material possessions. Each is equally troublesome: obsessive worry about not having enough or being consumed by desire for more. We should not value money so highly that it becomes the true "love" of our life.

Paul writes about the love of money in his First Letter to Timothy:

> **Now there is great gain in godliness with contentment, for we brought nothing into the world, and we cannot take anything out of the world. But if we have food and clothing, with these we will be content. But those who desire to be rich fall into temptation, into a snare, into many senseless and harmful desires that plunge people into ruin and destruction. *For the love of money is a root of all kinds of evils.* It is through this craving that some have wandered away from the faith and pierced themselves with many pangs. (1 Timothy 6:6–10, emphasis added)**

In these verses Paul states that discontent brings all sorts of trouble. The allure of money is great, and we may suffer greatly if we overvalue it. In his Second Letter to Timothy, Paul warns that in the days before Christ's return, people will be "lovers of money" (2 Timothy 3:2). Certainly we can see that in our consumer-oriented culture. Daily we are bombarded with messages—television, radio, the Internet—telling us we must have more. Driven by their desire to have more material possessions, some even overextend themselves financially through high credit-card debt or second (or third) mortgages. Worry, grief, and sadness are the certain results.

On the other hand, the blessing of contentment, being satisfied that our loving God meets all our basic needs, brings joy and happiness. Paul's words to Timothy recall the story of a man who lost everything, yet continued praising God. Job's words, spoken after the death of his children and servants, after the destruction of his property, show that all that we have or own comes from God. Following his tremendous loss, Job declared: "Naked I came from my mother's womb, and naked shall I return. The LORD gave, and the LORD has taken away; blessed be the name of the LORD" (Job 1:21).

Money Is Not Our Master

Jesus said, "You cannot serve God and money" (Luke 16:13). Promising more than we need, or tempting us with more than we have, are money's counterfeit claims. We are not to put our hope in wealth (1 Timothy 6:17). When we trust in the things of the world, we choke out the power of the Word (Matthew 13:3–9, 18–23). Trusting in our wealth makes an idol out of money and breaks the First Commandment. Coveting worldly possessions that we cannot afford breaks the Tenth Commandment. Loving money as our god, we open ourselves to a host of ills that can affect every area of our lives.

And yet, we join with Paul in declaring that God has "saved us and called us to a holy calling, not because of our works but because of His own purpose and grace" (2 Timothy 1:9). Through Christ's bloody cross and empty tomb, He has elevated us to a new relationship with Himself, so that "He might show the immeasurable riches of His grace in kindness toward us in Christ Jesus" (Ephesians 2:7). The kingdom of heaven—the forgiveness of sins and eternal life, which we have here and now in Jesus Christ—is of such inestimable worth that we would give up everything of this life in order to have it (see Matthew 13:44–46). In spite of how much we have, or do not have, we thank God that He provides us money, and in so doing provides for our basic needs.

Run for the Crown

© FRANCISCO CRUZ / SUPERSTOCK

Raising his arms in victory, Robert Cheruiyot crosses the finish line of the 107th Boston Marathon. Coming in at 2 hours, 10 minutes, and 11 seconds, the 24-year-old Kenyan's heart pommels his oxygen-starved lungs. Every nerve, every sinew, and every muscle aches from those 26 exhausting miles. His tired body seems to melt into the taut winner's tape. The ecstatic crowd screeches with delight. Robert Cheruiyot has made it to the finish, and he has won.

An athlete crossing a finish line is a powerful image. Paul draws on such an example from the world of athletics to describe the life of a Christian. God gives us the rules, the training, and the motivation we need to run the course set before us. He places us in the race and ensures that we complete it. In Christ, we run successfully, and we will receive our reward. A marathon runner races for his reward under his own power. Christians, however, are different. By the power of God's Word, we run for the crown.

© HUGH BURDEN / SUPERSTOCK

Following the Rules

Paul frequently uses examples from everyday life to highlight the Gospel for his hearers and readers. One example comes from athletics, particularly running (track). Like any race involving competitors, there are certain aspects of the race that must be followed. The first among these are the rules of the race. Paul writes, "An athlete is not crowned unless he competes according to the rules" (2 Timothy 2:5).

Paul wrote those words to encourage young pastor Timothy in his efforts to serve God's people. The Olympic Games held in Athens, and the Isthmian Games held in Corinth, were probably familiar to Timothy's congregation. These games had strict rules for athletes to follow. Likewise, Timothy, running his race as God's servant, will remain faithful in his calling (1 Timothy 4:6, 11; 6:20; 2 Timothy 4:1–2) and in his life (1 Timothy 4:16; 5:22; 2 Timothy 2:22–26). Timothy's parishioners, too, will follow the rules as they compete in life's race with humility, godliness, and love (1 Timothy 2:8–15).

Training for the Race

Another aspect of competition is the training involved. In the ancient games, athletes had to prove to game officials that they had trained for nearly a year prior to an athletic event. Athletes who had not trained were disqualified from participating in the race. In the Olympic Games, for example, athletes gave an oath that they had trained for at least 10 months. Athletes who were not self-disciplined and allowed to compete would lower the standard of the Games.

Paul points to his own track experience as an example. God's athletes train in God's Word. "You, however, have followed my teaching, my conduct, my aim in life, my faith, my patience, my love. . . . All Scripture is breathed out by God and profitable for teaching, for reproof, for correction, and for training in righteousness, that the man of God may be competent, equipped for every good work" (2 Timothy 3:10, 16–17). Through Law and Gospel, God provides the necessary training for every athlete to run and run well.

Running for the Crown

The third and final aspect of a Christian's race is the motivation for running. An athlete may be motivated by many factors: desire to compete, enjoyment of sport, prospect of an award. Paul indicates that a Christian, too, is motivated to run life's race with persistence and endurance. "I have fought the good fight, I have finished the race, I have kept the faith. Henceforth there is laid up for me the crown of righteousness, which the Lord, the righteous judge, will award to me on that Day, and not only to me but also to all who have loved His appearing" (2 Timothy 4:7–8).

Paul presents us with what awaits every believer at the "finish line": our reward, the crown of Christ's righteousness. Ancient runners received a crown of laurel leaves, which would last only a few days. Christ's crown lasts forever. We who have already been clothed with Christ's righteousness in Baptism (Galatians 3:27), and have been declared righteous through faith in Him (Romans 3:22), will receive this crown. It will be ours not because we participated in the race or ran well, but solely because Christ has already run the race for us and won (Romans 1:16–17; 8:29–30; Colossians 1:15–18).

Victory Ahead!

© BOB SHIRTZ / SUPERSTOCK

In our race, we often break the rules of God's Law or fail to train in His Word. By trusting in the rules that we make and easily follow, we become prideful. We try to justify ourselves before a holy and righteous God. We devise our own training schedule, which often appears religious but has nothing to do with God's Word. Our lack of discipline, evidenced by our thoughts, words, and deeds, proves we have taken our eyes off the prize. By running our own race according to our own rules, we will ultimately lose—eternally.

But Christ has called you to participate in the race in which He is already the Victor. He has already won the race for you! Although you are not a perfect athlete (Philippians 3:12), you are forgiven of your sins through Christ's blood. Christ Himself is your strength to endure to the end (3:13). He gives you the strength to strive for His prize (3:14). He waits for you and all the saints, ready to share His eternal glory (Colossians 3:1–4). "Everlasting joy shall be upon [your] heads; [you] shall obtain gladness and joy, and sorrow and sighing shall flee away" (Isaiah 51:11).

General Athletics

An athlete is not crowned unless he competes according to the rules.
2 Timothy 2:5

Let no one disqualify you, insisting on asceticism and worship of angels, going on in detail about visions, puffed up without reason by his sensuous mind, and not holding fast to the Head, from whom the whole body, nourished and knit together through its joints and ligaments, grows with a growth that is from God.
Colossians 2:18–19

CONTENDING FOR THE GOSPEL

Sports Stories in Paul's Epistles

Track

But I do not account my life of any value nor as precious to myself, if only I may finish my course and the ministry that I received from the Lord Jesus, to testify to the gospel of the grace of God.
Acts 20:24

Do you not know that in a race all the runners compete, but only one receives the prize? So run that you may obtain it. Every athlete exercises self-control in all things. They do it to receive a perishable wreath, but we an imperishable. So I do not run aimlessly; I do not box as one beating the air. But I discipline my body and keep it under control, lest after preaching to others I myself should be disqualified.
1 Corinthians 9:24–27

I went up because of a revelation and set before them (though privately before those who seemed influential) the gospel that I proclaim among the Gentiles, in order to make sure I was not running or had not run in vain.

You were running well. Who hindered you from obeying the truth?
Galatians 5:7

Do all things without grumbling or questioning, that you may be blameless and innocent, children of God without blemish in the midst of a crooked and twisted generation, among whom you shine as lights in the world, holding fast to the word of life, so that in the day of Christ I may be proud that I did not run in vain or labor in vain.
Philippians 2:14–16

Not that I have already obtained this or am already perfect, but I press on to make it my own, because Christ Jesus has made me His own. Brothers, I do not consider that I have made it my own. But one thing I do: forgetting what lies behind and straining forward to what lies ahead, I press on toward the goal for the prize of the upward call of God in Christ Jesus.
Philippians 3:12–14

I have fought the good fight, I have finished the race, I have kept the faith.
2 Timothy 4:7

Boxing

So I do not run aimlessly; I do not box as one beating the air.
1 Corinthians 9:26

Fight the good fight of the faith.
1 Timothy 6:12

I have fought the good fight, I have finished the race, I have kept the faith. Henceforth there is laid up for me the crown of righteousness, which the Lord, the righteous judge, will award to me on that Day, and not only to me but also to all who have loved His appearing.
2 Timothy 4:7–8

Slavery in the Bible

Her youthful eyes show centuries of slavery in her country. At age 37, Maalouma serves as the Bureau Chief of S.O.S. Slaves, an antislavery organization based in Mauritania, West Africa. Maalouma was born a slave. But now as a free woman she seeks to liberate countless men, women, and children still held captive in Mauritania and many other parts of the world.

Maalouma and the current plight of her enslaved fellow citizens might cause many Bible readers to recall a similar history of suffering, abuse, and grief experienced by many Africans two centuries ago—in North America. Because such memories are painful and haunting, understanding the words *slave* or *slavery* in Paul's Letter to Philemon requires that we do some research. This article will help you understand slaves' legal and social standing during Paul's day. With this knowledge and God's help, you will see how these scriptural passages dealing with this sensitive topic apply to you today.

Slavery in the Old Testament

The Scriptures neither endorse nor promote the practice of holding human beings as chattel, or the personal property of another. In fact, the Bible typically treats slavery in a negative light; "freedom" through God's saving grace is the dominant theme in both testaments. Held captive for 430 years under the hand of a cruel oppressor (Exodus 12:40–41), the Hebrew people cried to God for deliverance. God heard their cries and sent a leader to aid in their release from Pharaoh. Speaking to Moses from the burning bush, God said:

> I have surely seen the affliction of My people who are in Egypt and have heard their cry because of their taskmasters. I know their sufferings, and I have come down to deliver them out of the hand of the Egyptians and to bring them up out of that land to a good and broad land, a land flowing with milk and honey. . . . Come, I will send you to Pharaoh that you may bring my people, the children of Israel, out of Egypt. (Exodus 3:7–10)

Where the Bible speaks of slavery continuing among God's people (who were themselves slaves for nearly five centuries), slavery appears as a temporary allowance for human weakness rather than a perpetual divine right. Following the exodus, the Law of Moses permitted the holding of even Hebrew slaves, but only for a period of six years—slaves were to be released at the beginning of every seventh year. Bondage for life was to be only on a voluntary basis (Exodus 21:5–6). God's personal interaction with slaves seems to be one of kindness and compassion (see the story of Hagar and Ishmael in Genesis 21:8–21 and Jesus' healing of the centurion's servant in Matthew 8:5–13). God extended His grace, love, and sacramental forgiveness not only to free persons, but also to slaves (the covenant of circumcision in Genesis 17:1–14; the Passover in Exodus 12:44).

Slavery in the New Testament

In the New Testament, the Greek word for "slave" has a much broader meaning than what might be familiar to many Bible readers. In the Roman world, slaves could serve in a variety of positions (from chain gang to cook, from hairdresser to obstetrician). Roman slaves quite often held positions of great power and responsibility. In contrast to that practiced in the West, slavery in the Roman world was not associated with the oppression of any particular race. Slaves were most often prisoners of war taken from foreign lands, or non-Roman individuals sold by their families to repay a debt. Fair-skinned Britons and blond Germanic tribesmen were included in their number.

Typical Roman slaves hoped for release (manumission) at age 30, the usual age for discharge. While in service to their master, slaves could earn wages, buy and sell property, enter into contracts, and themselves own slaves. Not infrequently, Roman free persons sold themselves into slavery in order to pay debts, while non-Roman persons sold themselves in order to obtain eventual Roman citizenship. According to Roman law, upon his or her release a former slave was immediately considered a citizen of Rome.

In Paul's Letter to Philemon, the slave Onesimus appears to be a high-ranking personal servant entrusted with caring for his master's temporal possessions (having access to his money), an enviable position to hold. Paul's tenor in this short Letter is one of reconciliation and forgiveness: restoring the slave to a right relationship with his brother in Christ—who is also his earthly master—is the goal. Notably, in his First Letter to Timothy, Paul condemns those involved in "kidnapping" persons to be sold into slavery, listing "enslavers" among those especially deserving of the Law's condemnation (1 Timothy 1:10).

Joseph Sold into Egypt by James J. Tissot (1836–1902)

Work Today

With these things in mind, Paul's advice to slaves and to their masters does have import for contemporary Christians, particularly in regard to their workplace. Seen in the light of the modern employer/employee relationship, we find Paul encouraging each worker to remain faithful in their God-given calling and to their God-given employer (1 Corinthians 7:17, 21, 24); discouraging believing workers from accepting unsuitable or demeaning work (v. 23); advocating obedience and service to those in positions of authority (Ephesians 6:5–8; Titus 2:9); and reminding believers having temporal responsibility that they are not to abuse power with their subordinates, but to treat them kindly, remembering that they are accountable also to Christ (1 Corinthians 7:22; Ephesians 6:9).

Luther explains concerning the Fourth Commandment: "We should fear and love God so that we do not despise or anger our parents and other authorities, but honor them, serve and obey them, love and cherish them." God has given each one of us responsibilities of service, so that we may be a blessing to others. Regrettably, we often forsake those responsibilities and do injury to those in authority over us by disobeying their reasonable requests or by stealing from our employer through laziness or shoddy work. When we act in these ways, we are not behaving as free persons, but rather as slaves—slaves to sin (Romans 6:16).

"But thanks be to God, that you who were once slaves of sin . . . [have] been set free from sin, have become slaves of righteousness" (Romans 6:17–18). In Christ we have been delivered by God's mighty hand and outstretched arm, a hand and an arm that once were bound to a cross, but are now raised in blessing. God heard our cry for mercy and sent us a deliverer, one "worthy of more glory than Moses" (Hebrews 3:3), who has crushed the chains of oppression under His feet. In God's Son we are "free indeed" (John 8:36). Paul sums up who and what we are because of Christ in these words: "For freedom Christ has set us free; stand firm therefore, and do not submit again to a yoke of slavery" (Galatians 5:1).

Source: "Breaking Free from the Bonds of Slavery," *an interview with Maalouma Messaoud, slavery survivor and Mauritanian abolitionist, from* http://www.iabolish.com/act/abol/profile/maalouma3.htm.

SET

FREE TO SERVE

Born on Christmas Day, 1821, in Oxford, Massachusetts, Clara Barton was destined for service. At age 11, she nursed her brother David back to health following an accident. At age 15, she began a teaching career, which lasted nearly 20 years. At age 40, when the Sixth Massachusetts Regiment arrived in Washington, D.C., without its luggage, Clara organized a relief program. During the Civil War, Clara could often be found aiding the sick and dying, shells and smoke surrounding her. At age 60, she founded the American Red Cross (1881), retiring from her post as that agency's first president in 1904. The "Angel of the Battlefield" gave her entire life in service to her fellow man.

But where Clara Barton excelled in every way—in the home, in the schoolroom, and on the battlefield—many others have failed. The story of Onesimus is the story of every person who has fallen from grace, only to be raised back up again. In Christ, through Paul's ministry of reconciliation, both Philemon and Onesimus were restored to God and to neighbor. As such, their story becomes our story—the story of every Christian. Because Christ has set us free, we can serve others.

Understanding the Background

When you read Paul's brief Letter to Philemon (the Letter contains only 25 verses), you are immediately struck with Paul's conciliatory tone. He wants to present his case to Philemon in the most persuasive way. From the Letter, we learn that Onesimus served as Philemon's slave (see "Slavery in the Bible" for a discussion of this topic) and had run away. Onesimus had even stolen money (v. 18). Under Roman law, either offense was punishable by death, should the slave's owner so choose. We can imagine that this situation had caused problems within Philemon's home and within the congregation that met there to worship.

The situation was very unstable. Onesimus had been in Paul's company for some time, serving him during Paul's imprisonment. From the Letter we learn that, through Paul's preaching, Onesimus had come to faith in Christ (v. 10). Yet legally, he was still Philemon's slave. How Paul responded to this situation involving this believer—a runaway slave—was vitally important.

Restoration and God's Grace

Paul "appeals" (vv. 9–10) to Philemon to consider Onesimus not as a fugitive and a thief, but as a brother in Christ (v. 16). Clearly Onesimus had become close to Paul and had even aided him greatly in his ministry. Although in human chains, Paul experienced true freedom as a prisoner for Christ Jesus (v. 1). Paul wanted both Philemon and Onesimus to experience the freedom that only Christ can bring: reconciliation with God and reconciliation with those who have hurt us. To that end and on Onesimus's behalf, Paul sets asides his rights as an apostle (vv. 8–10) and promises to repay Philemon whatever was due him (vv. 18–19).

What Paul does for Onesimus reminded Philemon (and reminds us) of what Christ did for us by setting aside his divine rights (Philippians 2:6–8) and by fully paying our debt of sin (Colossians 1:13–14). Regarding the Second Article of the Apostles' Creed, Luther explains Christ's work this way:

> [Christ has] redeemed me, a lost and condemned person, purchased and won me from all sins, from death, and from the power of the devil; not with gold or silver, but with His holy, precious blood and with His innocent suffering and death, that I may be His own and live under Him in His kingdom and serve Him in everlasting righteousness, innocence, and blessedness, just as He is risen from the dead, lives and reigns to all eternity. This is most certainly true.

In Service to Others

In Roman culture, Paul's message of liberation, freedom, acceptance, and equality of all persons before God (see especially Galatians 3:23–4:7) would have especially resonated with Onesimus. As God's son and an heir of Christ, he would enjoy full legal standing within God's kingdom of heaven. Baptized "in one Spirit . . . into one body—Jews or Greeks, slave or free—and all were made to drink of one Spirit" (1 Corinthians 12:13), he would know that "Christ is all, and in all" (Colossians 3:11). What higher place or standing could a slave—or a free person, for that matter—attain?

In Christ, both Philemon and Onesimus could see each other in a new light: the light of the Gospel. Philemon could see his relationship with Onesimus as one in which he could serve Onesimus as a kind, generous, and fair master, or offer him employment as a free person. Onesimus, in turn, could continue to serve Philemon as a faithful servant or worker. Both could rejoice that their blood-bought freedom—from Satan, sin, and a certain death—would last forever, and that in spite of their "working" relationship, they shared equality in Christ. Their restored relationship, and uncoerced service motivated purely by love, was key, because it could show the congregation a beautiful picture of God's serving love in Christ (see Matthew 20:28; Galatians 5:13).

A New Master

God desires that we faithfully serve others having authority over us (Exodus 20:12; Ephesians 6:5–8), even fellow Christians, as we love our neighbors as ourselves (Matthew 22:39). Yet many times we refuse or deny this service. When we don't receive the recognition or the raise we deserve, our attitude can become bitter as our hearts become "enslaved" to hurt feelings and disappointment. By focusing on ourselves, we break not only the Fourth but also the First Commandment. And with sin as our master, we deserve God's certain condemnation and death.

Like Onesimus and Philemon, you, too, were enslaved to sin, death, and the devil. But you have been purchased and set free by the blood of Christ (Revelation 5:9). Your shackles of sin were severed by His cross! You have a new Master, whose "yoke is easy, and [whose] burden is light" (Matthew 11:30). By God's mercy, you were baptized into "a living hope through the resurrection of Jesus Christ from the dead, to an inheritance that is imperishable, undefiled, and unfading, kept in heaven for you" (1 Peter 1:3–4). Even with brothers or sisters who have wounded, hurt or disappointed you, you can still serve faithfully, because Christ has set you free!